What's the Worst That Can Happen?

Jessica Khan

[redacted]

ISBN 978-1-0980-6141-8 (paperback)
ISBN 978-1-0980-6142-5 (digital)

Christian Faith Publishing, Inc.
832 Park Avenue
Meadville, PA 16335
www.christianfaithpublishing.com

Printed in the United States of America

This is an absolutely true story about my life—how I grew up with a strict father, then moving to a small town and losing myself, having kids as a teenager, partying, and drinking every weekend. A tragedy accident happened that caused me to lean on drugs. Thoughts of suicide and deep depression had the best of me. I fell to my lowest point of my life until a great friend suggested that I come to church with her. That changed my life forever. I found God and his Holy Spirit. It motivated and gave me the will power to turn my life around. I hope this book will inspire the readers and help you deal with your problems in a better way. I know that someone can relate or knows someone who can relate to something in this book, whether it's alcohol, drugs, deaths, or child abuse. We all go through trials and tribulations in life. It's the way we handle them when it hits you in the face that matters. I recommend that you accept God in your life and start receiving your blessings.

Chapter 1

Growing up in a small town, Colorado City, Texas, (West, Texas). I'm the youngest out of eight children. As a child, you can say I was mischievous. I was always getting into things. I was just plain and simple, a bad little girl, but I had my reasons. My father was a strict man and targeted me more than my other siblings. Ever since I was a baby, my dad gave me the nickname "syrup." He said that he called me that 'cause when I was born, I was the color of syrup. Kids had a ball making fun of my name. I was syrup and biscuits, Karo syrup, anything they can think of I was called. But I got used to it and didn't care what the kids thought. It gave them something to talk about.

My brother Steve and nephew Ray and I grew up together. The rest of my brothers and sisters were grown and already on their own. Steve is a year older than me and Ray is my oldest sister's son, Sue. He and I were the same age. Momma used to dress us up alike, and people actually thought that we were twins. Sue had him in an early age. He was half Spanish. She started dating this other guy that didn't want a mixed child, so she left Ray with his father. His father couldn't raise him, so Momma took him in and raise him as hers. She said when she got him, he was about two, and he could talk. But he didn't know any English, and she didn't know any Spanish. So she would bring a friend to the house to translate, but eventually he learned English.

My dad owns a little juke joint, and sometimes he would take us there. It was fun sitting at the bar, watching grown people drink, and letting loose like they were children. My dad was a tall slender man that had shiny gold teeth, and the ladies had their eye on him. And he knew it too. He would wear his cowboy hat, his snake skin boots, and his Wrangler jeans. A lot of people respected him. He was always an upfront person with the charm of a serpent. He retired from his job because he had a bad heart and was trying for his disability. So he could afford to be up all night and run a bar and sleep all day. It was a different story for my mom. She took on two shifts from her job to pay bills 'cause his disability hasn't started yet. So she would only come to the juke joint whenever she could.

One day, we all were at the bar, and this lady from the neighborhood was dancing. All of sudden, my dad came right behind her grinding on her and whispering in her ear. I know I'm young (6 years), but I'm old enough to know that was wrong. This wasn't dancing. It looked like they were making love. I'm looking at my mom like, *Are you going to say something?* And him doing this right in front of his kids. My mom acted as if she didn't see it and looked the other way. Now my mother is a very beautiful woman. She has a light complexion, medium size, and looks like her grandma who was full Indian. Later on that night, when we were at home Steve, Ray and I went to bed. I was very tired. We been up all night at the bar, and I was sneaking beers when my parents weren't looking. So I went right to sleep; and in the middle of the night, I heard screaming and something hitting the walls.

I woke up Steve and said, "They fighting again." This was nothing new. They fought every weekend as far as I could remember, but it still scared us every time. So we woke up Ray and started to run. We left in our sleeping clothes barefooted. We ran to the neighbor house. They were used to us knocking on their door in the middle of the night. I don't know why we use to run to the neighbors. I guess we were scared of what daddy might do. When they opened the door, we told them they were fighting again, gasping for air. The neighbor husband went to our house to see what's going on. While we stayed at his house with his wife, she made us a pallet on the floor, and we stayed there until Momma got us the next morning.

Chapter 2

My mom wasn't a saint either. She used to take us out of town about thirty miles away from where we stay to meet this man named Charles. I like Charles. He was nothing like my dad. He would take the time and play with us and gave me the father attention I was looking for. Charles would take us out to eat and ask all kinds of questions. He was really concerned about our life and future. I just felt love when I was in his presence, and I just didn't get that from my dad. When we were leaving from our visit from Charles, I saw him give my mom money like he always does when we visit him. Every time, she would leave and get in the car and say the same thing over, "Don't tell your dad where we been. Tell him we were visiting my sister." I knew not to tell 'cause I didn't want to be the reason for them fighting, and Charles was so nice to us I didn't want to mess that up either.

My dad would be in different moods. One day, he's okay; and the next minute, he's not. I got whooped a lot, and he hardly ever whooped Steve or Ray. One day, we were playing mud ball fight at the bus stop a corner from the house, Steve and I against Ray and Shannon. Shannon is my niece who's two years under me. Her mom is the second oldest, and they stayed like thirty-five miles away. But she would come on the weekends. We were all throwing mud balls at each other and really having a good time until Ray had a rock in his mud ball and hit me right under my eye. It spit open soon as the impact hit me. I started bleeding very heavily. As I was walking to the house, a man and a woman saw me and saw all the blood. They stopped me and gave me a handkerchief to put over my eye to stop the bleeding. Then they put me in their car to take me home.

When we made it home, the good Samaritans took me to the door. My mom was at work, and I knew my dad get most of his sleep in the day time. When he opened the door, they were telling him that I might need to go to the hospital to get stitches. Steve, Ray, and Shannon was running to the house. When the good Samaritans left, Daddy told them, "Y'all get in the house, and y'all going to get a whooping." I'm thinking to myself, *I can sit this one down and watch while somebody is else getting a whooping for once.* He whooped them then came in my room and said, "Don't think you done got out of it, been your ass here." He tore me up worse than he whooped the others, bloody and all. I never seen a doctor. The scar heal up on its own, but we hardly ever go to the doctor unless it was really life-and-death emergency.

One day, I was sitting on the porch with Daddy, and we had a lot of goats and pigs. This one goat had a little baby. It was so cute. I told my dad I want him; and being a little girl, I wasn't thinking. All I knew is that the little goat was so adorable, and I could keep it as my own personal pet. He looked at me and said, "If you want it, go get him." That's my dad, and he is giving the okay to get the baby goat. So I ran and picked him up. As soon as I picked the baby goat up, the momma goat came charging and bucking at me. I ran as fast as I could, not letting go of the baby goat, and made it to our porch. My daddy was just laughing. He was so tickle. I'm young, not knowing the momma goat protected over her baby and was about to kill me. He stopped laughing and told me I had to let it go, and I didn't want to. So I started crying. He whooped me 'cause I started crying after he told me I could have it and almost dying. I guess he didn't think I was that fast and that the momma goat was going to whooped me. That was one of his ways of me learning my lesson.

One day, I got tired of getting whooped; so when he went to go get his leather belt with the big buckle on it, when he turned his back, I took off running straight out the back door. I didn't know where I was going. All I knew was I had to get away. I couldn't understand why was I the only target. I looked back, and he was right behind me with his cowboy boots and all. I didn't think he could run that fast because I never see him run. He caught up with me and tore my butt up all the way back home. After that, I became mischievous. I didn't care Steve would dare me to do something foolish like climb on top of the house and jump down, and I would do it. I would do anything without a question because I was going to get whooped anyways, so I made it worth it.

Chapter 3

Daddy had gotten another woman pregnant, and Momma was tired. They were cheating on each other for years; and with the fighting every weekend, she just couldn't do it anymore. So she wanted a divorce and move far away. They have been married over forty years. He used to beat on her and cheat throughout the relationship. She cheated too. The relationship was just toxic. And it was time for someone to leave, or someone was going to die. She packed Steve, Ray, and I, and we left with nothing but a few clothes. And she had little money from her paycheck. We started off going to Fort Worth. She has two sisters that stayed there. When we made it, we were lost. This was a big city compared to Colorado City. So she stopped at a payphone and called her sister, and her sister tried her best to explain where she stayed, but we were still lost. We rode around the city till close to dark, and we were getting on her nerves—three bad kids packed in the car for hours. She had gotten frustrated 'cause we were lost, and we were not making it any better fighting in the back seat. So she told us, "Change of plan." So we left Fort Worth and headed to a little small town named Calvert.

She had a brother who stayed there and lots of cousins; and that's where she was born, on a little farm on the outside of town. When we made it to Calvert, we stayed with our cousin, Aunt Mae until we can find our own home. She was our cousin, but we all call her Aunt Mae. She owns a bar in Calvert and Momma would go out with her. Momma went out every weekend, and we would stay with Aunt Mae's daughter who had kids our age. We found a house really fast. It was less than a month. So we went back to West, Texas, to get the rest of our belongings. When we made it to the house, Daddy was very happy to see us. He embraced us all with a hug, and I have never seen him this happy before. He said, "Syrup, y'all go visit y'all grandmother, so I can speak with your mother in private." Grandmother stayed a corner from the house, so we went on our way.

We made it about fifty feet from the house when I heard my mom yelling, "Call the ambulance." I looked at Steve and said, "they fighting again." We were so used to them fighting. It was routine to us. So we did what we always do and ran to the neighbor's house. The only thing that was different to me is that it was day time, and we usually run at night. And they didn't seem to be drunk. We stayed with the neighbor's wife, and her husband went to see what was going on like always.

A few minutes went by, and I heard the ambulance. Do I ran back to our house to see what happened? When I got there, the neighbor was doing CPR on my dad. Then the paramedics took over. I will never forget the look on my father's face as he lying on the floor with his eyes rolling into the back of his head. This strong man that had so much respect from everybody was now looking so helpless. We all looked confused 'cause I thought they were fighting, even my mom looked confused. The ambulance took him to the hospital. Now we know that he had a heart attack. He just had heart surgery. That's how he got his disability started. Not even an hour of being in the hospital, he died. We later learned that he predicted his death. He told everyone in town that as soon as my mom come to get her things, he was going to see his family and die. I guess he believed that so much that it actually came true. He told people that he couldn't live without his wife and his family. It's so crazy how they would fight so much and cheat on each other, but he still couldn't see his life without her.

At the wake, all my family on my daddy's side met at our grandma's house. There were so many people there, and I heard my aunt (my dad's sister) crying and saying, "She did it. I know she had something to do with it." I was too young to understand, but now I know that they blame Momma for his death. She was his wife, and they fought all the time. But she still loved him and wouldn't have done anything to hurt him. His family did his obituary, and they put all his other kids he had on the side before her kids. They had his mistress sitting in the front row with her. They just treated her so badly, spiteful for no reason. How can you kill someone that had a heart attack? And he had heart problems for years. She couldn't grieve because she felt so much hate surrounding her. After the funeral, we left West, Texas, and went back to our home in Calvert. She said she never wanted to come back to West, Texas. After daddy's death, I used to wake up every night with nightmares that he would come back to get me. Even though he treated me different from the others, he was still my dad, and I did love him. His death had an effect on me.

CHAPTER 4

Calvert was very different from Colorado City. It was much smaller population of maybe 1200, so everybody knew everybody. You really didn't need a car. Most of the people walk around, kids and all. Even the schools were different in West, Texas. There were a mixture of race, but here it was segregated. There were nothing but blacks and the white students went to a private school. The whites stayed on one side of the tracks and the blacks stayed on the other side. When I went to school, my classmates would say, "You sound like a white girl." Whatever that means. I adjusted really fast here. I thought I was bad, but I had nothing on these kids. They were the real deal and that made me slow down, and I wasn't getting a whooping every day either.

For a couple months, I kept having those same nightmares of Daddy coming back for me. After his death, Momma told me that the man we used to visit, Charles, was my and Steve's dad. Charles was married and so was she. That's why they used to sneak around. Now it make sense. That's why he always felt like a father figure, and he used to give my mom money to take care of us every time we visit. Maybe that's why the man I thought was my dad used to whoop me all the time 'cause he knew that I wasn't his child. My mom found a new man named Jeff. She met him years ago when she used to come here to visit her brother. They had been friends but never pursue a relationship until now. I was happy Momma had a man that didn't whoop us and treat us like we were his. He worked Mondays through Fridays; and on the weekends, he like to drink.

They both liked to drink. One night, she came home drunk, and Steve was about ten at the time. He told her, "We just lost our daddy, and our mom ain't nothing but an alcoholic. We going to lose you too." That hurt her feelings, but sometimes the truth hurts. And she promise she would stop drinking. But that didn't stop Jeff. He continued to drink. His brother owns a bar, and sometimes he wouldn't come home on the weekends. Momma was trying to change her life. She quit drinking due to her diabetes and high blood pressure and her promise she made to Steve. She started going to church and joined. When she went up to the altar, I was right behind her. I was really young to understand, but I knew it made her happy. She even tried to quit cursing, and I know that was hard to do because she talked like a mad sailor. We went to church for a couple more months, then we just stopped. Every now and then, we would go maybe for holidays.

That summer, Charles wanted me to come to his house and stay the summer vacation with him and his family. I was scared because I met him, but I didn't know him personally. And I never met his wife or his other daughter, Shun, who's around the same age as me. So I asked if Shannon could come with me. Her mom is the second oldest sister, and she just moved to Calvert to get a fresh start with her three kids. Shannon is the oldest, and she's just two years under me, so we always had a close bond. They agreed that it was okay for her to come too. They all were so kind to me and Shannon his wife didn't treat us no different. I can just imagine the hurt she felt knowing that I was conceive while she thought she was in a happy marriage. My mom and her was pregnant at the same time. Seeing them together was inspiring. They show me how a happy couple should be like. I've never seen my mom this happy, not even with her new boyfriend Jeff. It's nice having a little sister, and I had more older sisters and brothers that I met from his first wife.

When I came back home, things went back to normal. Months passed, and it was close to Christmas. Momma bought some lights to put up, and she wanted them to go on top of the house. She was going to pay someone, but Steve said he could do it. She thought he was too young and didn't want him to, but he persisted that he could do it so she let him. He put them up with no problem and climb down from the ladder. He told me, "Let's play a joke on Momma. Tell her I fell." Momma went inside the house when she saw Steve get on top of the house with no problem. So I said okay at the time. I thought it was a good idea. I put my best actress role on and ran in the house with my serious look on, yelling "Momma, momma." She was in the kitchen washing dishes. She looked up at me, and I didn't give her time to answer. I told her Steve fell. She looked shocked and scared at the same time. So she followed me out the door. The next thing I knew she had passed me up. Steve was lying on the ground, moaning on the ground like he was really hurt. She picked his head up saying, "Oh, my baby." Then Steve burst out laughing. She dropped him and came charging at me, hitting me all across the head telling me, "You crazy kids going to give me a heart attack." I tried to tell her it was Steve idea, but she wasn't trying to hear me. And now Steve was laughing at me cause I'm the one getting hit.

That Christmas, we had so many presents under the Christmas tree. I have never seen so many presents in my life under one tree. I was so happy because most of them had my name on them. Girls always get more than boys. Christmas day, I was so excited to open them; but when I opened them, I was sad. I wanted to cry because all of them came from the yard sale. I had some dirty-looking shoes, used clothes, and a whole lot of naked barbie dolls. I was young and didn't understand the situation. All I knew that it was Christmas, and I have all these used items. My mom wasn't working. She filed for her disability, and the only income we had to rely on was Jeff's paycheck that we needed for the bills. I now know she did her best, but she had me fooled with all that pretty wrapping paper.

CHAPTER 5

Now I'm in high school, and things have changed a lot since I was younger. I used to be bad, do and say anything I wanted too. Now I was all shy, and it's hard to express myself if I didn't know you really well. I didn't have many friends, so I just hung around my niece Shannon. Ray took on this bad-boy, want-to-be-gangster persona. So Shannon and I would try to imitate him, but I couldn't 'cause I was so bashful. We still pretend we were these gangster girls that smoke weed all day. On the weekend, Shannon would stay with us. One evening, we were walking to the store. As we got closer to the store, we saw Ray coming out the store, running fast across us. So we went behind him to see what's going on. We met him in an alley across from the store. One of his friends was already there, waiting on him. They were taking turns going in the store stealing forty-ounce bottle of beers. So I told him I wanted one and Shannon said, "Me too." So they got us some, and we sat right there in the alley and smoked weed and got drunk.

We wobble to the house, Momma made some fried fish, and Shannon fixed her a big plate and ate it all so fast. Soon as we lay down, she threw up everywhere. I tried to hurry and clean it up before Momma could smell the alcohol. She looked in my room, and said "Look at her greedy ass. She done ate so much and now puking everywhere." She never knew that we were drunk. The next day, she woke us up early in the morning to hang out clothes on the line, and Shannon was dragging around. Momma told her to "get your lazy butt up and help that girl." We started laughing because she didn't know Shannon had a hangover. I had an hangover too, but I could handle mine a little better. And this wasn't my first time drinking.

Steve didn't smoke weed, but he loved to drink. Momma brought him a car, so he could drive us to school. So one day, we were in school, and I saw Steve and a couple of his buddies piled up in his car. I ran out to the car 'cause I knew he was going to skip the rest of the day, and I wanted to skip too. He said "Syrup, no. Go back. You can't go." I told him that I was going to tell Momma. But he knew I wasn't going to tell. Something that we didn't do was tell on one another. He skipped school and got drunk for the rest of the day, and we didn't see him later on that night.

Every day after school, Shannon and I would walk around and get high. Today was different. I really didn't think about boys until this point. "They he go. He's going to be my husband one day," that's what I would tell Shannon. His name was Joe. We used to walk around and follow him. You can say stalk him. Joe was a little older than I, and he dropped out of school. He did what most of the boys from Calvert did his age, sold dope on the corners. He was bad-boy type, and that's what made me want him more. I was scared to talk to him; and one day, we passed cross each other, and Shannon told him I liked him. I bumped her like I was mad, but really I was screaming inside.

He said, "What's up, lil momma?" And we began to talk. We dated for a while. We had to sneak around, but it was nice. He would give a crackhead some dope, and they would rent out their house for an hour or two so we could meet up. I was so in love. I can't believe it. Life was just perfect.

One day, I went to school, and I couldn't stay awake. I couldn't remember the last time I had a period. I'm thinking to myself, *I know I'm pregnant and how can I hide this from my mom*. Now, my mom is a strong lady. Her and Daddy fought all the time—well, the man I thought was my dad. She will kill me if she knew I was pregnant, and I already decided that I want to keep my baby. Plus no one doesn't have any money for an abortion. So I'm going to hide it the best I can and wear bigger clothes. Try my best not to give away any signs.

Chapter 6

My mom's sister, Aunt Fae, moved in with us, the one she would tell us to say we were over her house when she was creeping. She was a Christian, a strong believer, her and her two children (they were not children a little older than us). She didn't wear pants, didn't watch BET, and I never heard her curse. But something happened in the church, something with the preacher. She didn't like to talk about it; but whatever it was, it made her lose her faith. So she moved with us to get a fresh start. She had this dog that she had for years with her and she loves this dog. Every time you see her, there was that dog. She had him trained and had a strong bond with him. One day, the dog followed Steve and got lost, or someone stole it. We looked for that dog everywhere for two days, and he never came back. She was so heartbroken. The demon was released. She started listening to blues and cursing. I was shocked to hear her curse for the first time. After that, her and my mom were acting like little teenagers. They were going out every weekend; and in the day time, they would laugh and enjoy each other's company.

Aunt Fae was the one that gave my mom the idea that I might be pregnant. She told my mom, "That girl's neck sure is getting long, and she's looking pale." I'm saying to myself, *Shut the hell up*. My baby bump was getting bigger, but I was hiding it with big clothes. She realized that she hasn't bought me any pads in a while. She asked me, and I told her I didn't know. I was lying the whole time. She didn't know I was having sex, and I told her I had done it once. So we went to the grocery store to get me a pregnancy test. I peed on that stick while her and my aunt stayed right there watching. It came back positive real quick. I started to cry. I wasn't ready to face the truth. She was cursing and was so mad, my aunt pumping her up, telling her, "I told you, sister. I told you that girl was pregnant." I thought she was going to put me out.

She told me to call Charles, my dad, and tell him the news 'cause she didn't know what to do with me. When I called him, I sounded like a little girl on the phone. I was sobbing so hard I couldn't get my words out. He said, "What's wrong, baby?"

And I said, "I… I… I'm pregnant." He told me it's done, and the only thing to do now is to make the best of it. And he talked with my mom. I felt a little relief 'cause that was the most positive thing I heard in a while. When my mom got off the phone, he must have gave her some of that positive energy 'cause she was much calmer. She told me she would be there for me, and I can finish school (I was just a freshman), and she would help with the baby.

I knew I was pregnant the whole time, but I didn't tell Joe. I didn't know how he would react. Now that it's out in the open I decided to tell him. So my mom took me over to his house to tell him the good news so we could be this happy little family. When I told him the news, he looked at me like I had crap on me. I started crying, and my mom got out of the car and told him, "My daughter is pregnant, and you are the daddy. What are you going to do?" He looked at my mom the same way. He never said a word just looking all dumb like he had no concern in the world. My mom said, "Just forget about this fool. He ain't about nothing anyways. I'll help you take care of this baby." I just couldn't believe this. This boy and I have been going strong ever since we started dated, and now he's acting like he doesn't know me. I don't know about him, but I was really in love. It's only been seven months we been together, and I'm now five months pregnant. We were together every day. I was so hurt. I didn't know what to do.

I had my mom and my aunt's support. They had so many rules and superstitions that I never heard of before. Sometimes I was thinking they were making things up as time went by. "No swiping. No lifting your hands over your head and no salt all kind of things. I was just a teenager, but I really appreciate the advice and concerns. I had my advantages because they would take turns cooking for me. Momma and Jeff relationship's wasn't getting any better either. She was tired of him after all the crap she put up with her husband and still taking crap from men. So they split up, and she started dating this guy named Al. Al treated her so kind. He catered to her every need. They walked in parks. He would take her out to eat, went on trips, and he love taking her to the casino on the weekends. They were such a cute couple. I have never seen her so happy, and he had a good bond with all of her kids. I just wish she would've met him much sooner 'cause he's the positive father figure I needed in my life. Charles is a good man, but he is a married man. And I didn't spend much time with him, so I didn't have that role in my life.

Chapter 7

I was sitting in class and this new student named Bill came in. His dad was dating this lady down the street from my house. All day long, Bill was staring at me; and I'm thinking to myself, *What the hell is he looking at? He never seen a pregnant girl before? I'm not trying to date anyone right now especially with my situation. I know he sees this big belly*. At this time, about seven months pregnant, and my baby bump is sticking way out there. His persistence broke me, and I gave in and decided to give him a chance. He was the opposite of Joe. He was shorter and darker, and I wasn't as attracted to him as I was with Joe. But I gave him a chance 'cause he was really a nice guy, and he was willing to be with me and take my unborn child as his own. There's no way Joe and I were getting back together. He was caught selling dope, and they sentenced him ten years. Couple months later, the school let me out on maternity leave because it was close to my due date.

My mom came home from her vacation with Al because she wanted to be there when I delivery. I started having contractions, and Momma took me straight to the hospital. I was finally about to have my baby. Bill was right there by my side. He was just as scared as I was. I was in the delivery room, looking across at him, and the nurses putting patches on him to monitor his heart. I started laughing and said to myself, *It's not even his baby, and he was freaking out.* That made me love him more. I was in labor for about twelve hours. I finally had my beautiful baby boy. I named him De'vonte. He is the most beautiful baby I have ever seen. He has these amazing hazel brown, gold-looking eyes, and a head full of silky black hair. He's so tiny in my arms. From that moment on, I knew I was going to love him forever. Bill embraced De'vonte just like he was his.

When I brought him home, he had his days and nights mixed up. He stayed up all night. Momma helped me out. We would take turns sleeping. She got sick with her diabetes, and the hospital kept her. After having De'vonte, I couldn't eat; and I, myself, felt really bad. But I just pushed the pain away until Momma comes home. I started getting this really bad smell down there, and I knew I was bathing and doing as the doctor said. But the smell was horrible. Steve was going out with this older girl, and she has kids. So I bend to her and told her I haven't been eating and developed this bad smell. She told me, "Well, you just had a baby, and you are bleeding all the time. So you going to have a smell." So I just put it to the back burner and tried to take care of my baby the best I could. They kept Momma in the hospital almost two weeks. When she came home, I told her what I was experiencing and that I was feeling weak. She tried to look up me; and when I opened my legs, I smell like death. It was a bad smell. I had stitches when I had De'vonte, and they have already dissolved on their own. She told me she couldn't see anything, but that smell was not normal. So she wanted to take me to the clinic.

When I made it to the clinic, I was so weak. It felt like I was going to pass out any second. I told the nurse what was going on and was waiting in the waiting room. The doctor came out really fast and asked me again what was going on, and I told him. He told my mom to take me to the emergency room now. He said, "With her just now having a baby, it could be anything or life and death." The way he was talking, it scared me, so we went right to the hospital. They took me to the back fast, and I had to get out of my clothes and put on a gown. I was so embarrassed. I could hear the nurses as they walk by saying, "What is that smell? Somebody needs to take a bath."

When the doctor came in, he found out the problem fast. My OB doctor left some gauzes inside of me. It was black-looking and smelled so bad. The doctor had a shock look on his face when he pulled them out of me. He asked who was my doctor and put me on some antibiotics and told me I could douche. I think that gauze had mildew inside of me, making me sick; and I do believe if my mom would have stayed one more week, she would've found me dead.

After the antibiotics and a little vinegar, I started feeling like myself again and started eating regularly.

After having De'vonte, I went back to school, and my mom and aunt helped with him. Months passed, and it was the summer. Momma wanted to go out of town with Al. I told her to go have fun. She don't have to quit living her life because I had a baby, plus I got tired of her and my aunt telling me to do this or do that. The more I tried, the more I heard, "He's hungry," "He need changing," etc. I really got offended, and I told them, "This is my baby. I know how to care for him." So momma left with Al, and De'vonte developed this bad cough. And it was getting worst. I called my Aunt Fae who was now living across town. I called her to pick us up and take us over to her house. When we were over her house, she said this baby sick, and she picked him up and said he's burning up with fever. She checked his temperature, and it was 104. And she called the ambulance. Before the ambulance came, De'vonte's fever had gotten so high. He started having a seizure, and his eyes were rolling in the back of his head. He was shaking in my arms. I started crying. I didn't want to lose my baby. That's all I was thinking.

The paramedic came, and we got in the ambulance. They were rubbing him down with alcohol pads, trying to get his fever down. The hospital finally got it down and ran all kind of tests on him, but they didn't find anything. We were there all night, and they said he had a bad cold and his fever got extremely high. That's what caused the seizure. On the way home, my aunt told me, "See, you trying to be grown. We just telling you things to help you. We not trying to tell you how to raise your child. We already had children and know what you are going through. We just trying to help you. That's all." After that, I welcomed any advice anyone has to give me. And I realized that I'm not in this alone and they love my baby just as much as I do.

Chapter 8

Steve was going out with this girl, and they had a baby boy named Jim. Jim was a couple months under De'vonte. Momma loves all her grandkids, but she always had them two when she wasn't with Al. Couple years passed, and I graduated. I was so happy I had my boys, De'vonte, Jim, my mom, and even Charles came from West, Texas, to be there. After graduation, I started looking for a job right away and found one, cleaning the college student restrooms. Every student I was cleaning up for was way older than I was. I graduated at seventeen because Momma changed Ray and my age up so we can start school early. This should've been me in school somewhere. But I have a child to take care, and I knew what I was doing. So it was time to woman up, and I wanted to help Momma with the bills.

One day, I was at home, washing dishes, and De'vonte walking around now, getting to everything. He's in the living room, playing with his toys. It got quiet, so I went in the living room to see what he was doing. And the front door was wide open. I ran outside yelling his name. I ran all around the house in a panic. I knew he like playing with our dog, but I didn't see him either. I'm nervous and started to shake. Thoughts came to me like, *Do you think someone came and kidnapped him?* I was just about to call the police when I saw one of the boys, that be on the corner selling dope, walking with De'vonte and the dog. Some kind of way, he opened the door, and I don't know what made him go to the corner. Was he following the dog? Or was the dog following him? The guy told me he was standing on the corner and saw a little baby walking down the street with a dog beside him. He said, at first, he thought he was tripping; but when they got closer, he knew it was De'vonte. He told me he just wants to chill on the block like his daddy. I was so mad but happy at the same time. I couldn't whoop him. I knew he was young and probably didn't understand, but I told him to listen to me, "You are not going to be like your daddy." I know I'm not perfect, but I want better for my child, and I would do anything to make sure he had whatever he needs.

Couple months later, Al got sick and I went with Momma to take him to the hospital. Al had emphysema before they met, but it has gotten worse. He barely can make it from the house to the car without losing his breath. He kept his asthma pump with him at all times. He told us that when he was younger, he would smoke three packs of cigarettes a day. After the army, he was nervous all the time. Now all that smoking has caught up with him. I felt so sorry for him gasping for air. The doctors said he had pneumonia, and that's not good with his emphysema. They had him on ventilator machine. He stayed in a coma for a week. But his body couldn't take it, and he died. Al dying hurt Momma. This was her time for happiness, but it was cut way to short. We buried him at a military cemetery. They gave Momma a pilot for the spouse; and she told me when she dies, she wanted to be buried in her white dress. She wanted me to do her hair and to be buried right next to Al. She really loved him and didn't want to date any more.

Most of my siblings moved to Calvert or close to here. Two more brothers Greg and Adam moved to Bryan, Texas which is thirty miles from Calvert. My oldest sister Sue who is Ray's mom moved to Calvert with her other two kids. I started working at the nursing home as a CNA. Sue worked there and got me on. It was better because it was right there in Calvert. Sue is very tall, about six feet, and very pretty, slim with a light complexion. If you see her, you would think she had Chinese in her 'cause she has these tight eyes and kept long hair in her head. She was very blunt, says whatever that was on her mind. But she's was very cool, easy to get along with, and working with her made my job easy. People have asked, "How can you work at a nursing home cleaning up boo-boo?" I tell them you get used to the smell. I actually get a joy out of helping people, especially the ones that can't help themselves. Someone has to do it.

One night, the nursing home threw a Christmas party for the staff. All of us in one room, whites and blacks, all partying and getting drunk together. Everyone was drunk; and to me, white people sure know how to party. My charge nurse Tina and I clicked like that. I had so much fun. Ever since the Christmas party, Tina have been wanting me to take her out to the bar in town on the black side. So I took her out. I'm thinking, *Since she's the only white person in this whole building she would feel uncomfortable.* Boy, was I wrong. She got loose, was on the dance floor and everything. I can't lie. She had no rhythm, but she sure looked like she was having a good time. Every weekend after that we would go out. We had our own little clique, Shay and Nita. They worked with us at the nursing home. Shay's sister, Jesse, Sue, Tina, and I, every weekend, we were out.

Chapter 9

Bill and I separated. We just went two different ways, but we remained friends. The whole time I was with him, I didn't get pregnant. Soon as we broke up, boom, I'm pregnant. I wasn't in a relationship because I just came out of a committed relationship with Bill. I was just messing around. While I was pregnant, I continued to work at the nursing home, but I stopped going out and drinking. One day, I was off, and De'vonte was in daycare. And momma wanted to go shopping in Bryan. She woke me up early in the morning, knowing I'm not a morning person, but I got up anyways. We did our shopping; and when we were done, she wanted to get something to eat. So we decided to go to Golden Corral buffet. That was okay with me. I was pregnant and eating for two. We must have ate like pigs. I had some of everything. When we got ready to go, she asked if I wanted drive; and I told her, "No, I wanted to go to sleep." I woke up, bouncing up and down. I looked around. We were going down into a bridge to a little pond. I looked at Momma, and she was asleep too. I was scared, so I screamed, "MOMMA." She woke up and stopped the car. We were stuck in the mud feets from the water. A man that we knew from town stopped and helped us out the hole. We laughed after it was over. I told her next time we go out and eat, she's not driving.

Momma caught a bad cold. She's coughing up green-looking mucus, and it getting worse. I told her I'm taking you to the hospital. When we made it there, they saw her right away. We didn't have to wait long. They ran all kinds of tests on her. About two hours later, the doctors came back and said she had pneumonia. They did an x-ray on her lungs. And the results came back that there was too much fluid in her lungs, and they wanted to keep her overnight. She told me to go, and I agreed. I was drained. We have been there all night, and I had to get De'vonte from over Shannon's house. So I told her, "Okay, I'll see you tomorrow." The next day, I got up and gathered all her things that I thought she would need—her gown, toothbrush, lotion, her house shoes, and a couple puzzle books. When I made it to the hospital, I walked into her room. It was empty. I thought maybe they took her out to run more test on her, so I waited. After waiting about thirty minutes, I went to the nurses' desk and asked them what happened to my mother. They told me that they had to move her to ICU because her condition had gotten worse, and her lungs were collapsing.

I went to the ICU area. But they wouldn't let me see her because they had a certain time that you could visit the patients, and they just had their visitation. So I had to wait for the next visiting time. I called all brothers and sisters to give them the news. Greg was already at the hospital 'cause he worked there as a daytime surgeon. He met me at the ICU waiting room. I had to go, so I could pick De'vonte up from daycare. Greg said he was going to visit her when it's time. The next day, I came back. Adam and Steve were there. They only let two visit at a time, so Steve and I went together. Adam said he had seen her that morning. When we made it to the room, my heart just broke. They had her on a ventilator. She had all kinds of tubes in her nose and mouth. They had her sedated, so she couldn't talk. It was like she was in a coma. All I was thinking was Al with the same ventilator, and he didn't make it. I just cried and grab her hand. I told her, "Come back, come back, Momma." I didn't know if she heard me or not.

A week later, Greg called me and said we all need to come to the hospital. When I got there, they said they had to put a tracheostomy in her neck. They said it was fluid going into her lungs, and Adam signed off for it 'cause he was the power of attorney. After they did the trachea. Her progress was better. They wanted to send her to a rehab center that worked on trachea patients. The closest rehab center was about two hours away. Two days later, Steve, Adam, and I went to go visit her; and when we got there, we were so surprised Momma was sitting up and trying to talk to us. It just sounded like she was whistling. It was so funny. I was so happy just to see her up and moving.

I said laughing, "Momma, what are you doing up?". The doctors said they were going to put some kind of device in her trachea so she could talk tomorrow. They also wanted to give her a water test to see if it was going into her lungs. She was on a restricted diet and have a feeding tube. She couldn't eat or drink nothing through her mouth but ice.

So the next day, we went back, and she was talking. It sounded funny hearing her talk through that pipe, but we were able to understand her. She asked whose decision was it to get her neck cut. We told her Adam. She looked at him with this mean look, and he responded, "Well, I wasn't going to let you die." We were just so happy to see her sitting up and talking. Then the doctor came in for the water test. She drunk the water and didn't choke, so she passed. He told us he would try solid food tomorrow and see how she will do. When the doctors left, she told us she has been drinking water ever since she came to the center. She said she was thirsty and tired of eating ice chips, so she would sneak in the restroom and sneak water. She didn't stay in the rehab long. She passed all her tests, and they took the trachea and the feeding tube out. And things went back to normal.

Chapter 10

After the scare with Momma, things with back as normal life. Months passed, and I had my beautiful baby girl named De'venna. She's light-skinned with thick hair. She looks like a baby doll in my arms. De'venna's dad and I were just friends. He was Steve's classmate. She was conceived on a drunken night. When I brought De'venna home, I was ready to stay up all night because when De'vonte was a baby, he stayed up all night and day. De'venna was different. She was a good baby. She slept most of the time. After having De'venna, I went back to work and back going out while Momma babysitted. Tina had a van; and before we would get off work, we'll buy some beer and have it iced down. About the time we got off work, it would be nice, cool, and ready. Tina was the wild one out of the group. Once she starts drinking, she gets loose. Shay was the chill—like me, quiet—but if you get out of line with her, she will let you know. Jesse was the man-eater in the bunch. She likes to make bets. "Let's see who can get this one first." She likes having fun with the situation. Nita was the serious one with the heart of gold. Tracy was the crazy one. She always finds herself in a fight at the end of the night, but she's a sweet girl and loyal friend, just sensitive to what everybody has to say. When we are all together, you would swear we were on weed or had some laughing gas 'cause we would laugh all night. We knew how to have a good time, and we loved each other like sisters.

One night, we (Shay, Tina, and I) had to work that morning and someone had a party out of town. So we decided to go, but to come home early. We partied all night long and forgot about time. Before we knew it, it was 5:00 a.m., and we had to be at work at 6:00 a.m. It took us about thirty minutes to make it back to Calvert. We went to Shay's house and put on some of her work clothes, drop the others off at their homes and rush to work. When I stepped out of the van, I looked at Tina, and Shay said, "I'm still drunk." We all started laughing. They said they were too. We went in and made it through the day. I was so tired, but I pushed through the day. When I made it over to my mom's house, she was mad 'cause I didn't pick the kids up, but I didn't hear her because I passed out. And the next week, we were at it again.

Couple months later, I met this Indian man who had a crush on me. We went out on a few dates, and he wanted me to marry him and move to Houston with him. Things were just moving too fast. We have only been dating three months, and my heart wasn't really in it. He was a nice guy. He wasn't like any other I had before. He provided for me and my kids and treated me like a queen. Momma told me. "Girl, you better marry that man. He got money, and you not going to find someone here that's going to take of you. And you can learn to love him." So we got married and I moved to Houston. Within three months, as a married woman I was ready to come back home. Things were different when we used to date; and moving in together, I miss my family and friends and partying, so I came back home. I felt bad hurting him because he was a good man, but I was too young and married for the wrong reason.

Chapter 11

I come back home and had to celebrate with the girls, so we went out. My cousin Kel from Houston was with us. Every time he comes to town, we would party. It's a funny story how we met. One night, I was at the bar, and I was feeling good. They played my song, so I went on the dance floor. This guy came behind me, and we were really getting it. After we got done dancing, we introduced ourselves. He asked me for my number, so I gave it to him. Then Steve came over toward us; and Kel told Steve, "I'm going to marry this girl." Steve started laughing but a little too hard, and I asked Kel, "How do you know my brother Steve?"

He said, "Your brother? That's my cousin." Steve continuously laughed, saying, "I was trying to tell y'all." We all started laughing; and ever since then, we have been close. So that night, I came back home from Houston. We all went out, and Kel was the hype man. He motivated us to go out in Bryan; and as soon as we made it, he went to sleep and didn't want to get out the car. So Shay, Nita, Jesse and I went in. Tina didn't come because she had a date at home, but she let me use her van.

We were having a good time. Dudes were trying to holla at us all night. The DJ was trying to talk to me. He bought us beer all night. Before I knew it, they were calling last call for alcohol, so we got our last beers and drunk them. After the club closed, everybody went outside and mingled. So we were all outside; and the DJ still tried to talk to me, so I walked with him to his car and gave him my number. I came back where Shay and Jesse were, and I asked, "Ae y'all ready to go?"

They said, "Yeah."

I asked them, "Where is Nita?"

And they said, "She probably in the van with Kel." So we got in the van, and Kel was still asleep. And Nita wasn't in there. Jesse said she probably met someone at the club and left. I didn't want to leave her; and if Nita would've met someone, she would've told us that she was leaving. So we got out again; and this time, we walked around the whole club looking for her. There were still a lot of people out there sitting on their cars and mingling around, but no Nita.

As we were walking back past the club, I heard knocking. I told Shay, "I bet that's Nita locked in the club." As we got closer, I was shouting her name.

She started yelling, "GET ME OUT OF HERE," in a panic, beating and kicking the door.

I told her, "Calm down. We here and going to get you out." I really didn't know how we were going to get her out. The owners have a big dead-bolt lock on the door. Then I remembered I have the DJ's number. He has to know the owners. So I called him, and he said they were on their way.

She told me "It's dark in here, and I'm scared."

I told her to "feel around and see if you can find a light switch and to relax. You in there with all that beer." She found the beer, and that made her much calmer. When the owners came, he looked shocked; and I'm thinking to myself, *I bet this has never happened before*. When he opened the door, Nita had drunk about six beers.

He said, "I see you found the beer." And we all started laughing. Nita was so happy to get out of there. She gave us a big hug, and we got in the van and left. We laughed at her the whole ride home.

I asked her, "How did you get locked in there? I thought we all left after last call for alcohol." She said after they called last call, she went to the restroom. While she was using the restroom, someone turned the lights off. She said she thought someone was playing; but when she was done and open the door, everything was dark. We laughed all night at Nita.

Chapter 12

Steve started going out with this girl named Diana right after his ex had Jim. They have been together for years and have a daughter together. They used to fight all the time, and I find myself wondering, *How can he fight his girlfriend after seeing what Momma went through*. But Diana was a firecracker too. He left and went out of town, so Shannon and I decided to take her out to the club. Before we went out, we stopped at a store and bought some beer. Shannon couldn't drink because she was pregnant, but Diana and I drank her share. We parked at the club, but I didn't want to get out until I finished my beer. So we sat in the car. Diana told me she had to pee; and I said, "Me too. We still have beer to finish, so let's drive around the corner and take a squat." I found a dark road just a few blocks away from the club and turned the lights off.

Shannon stayed in the car. Diana and I got right out and started releasing ourselves. I was in the middle of peeing when I saw headlights coming our way. I told Diana, "Here comes a car."

She said, "I can't stop."

"Me neither." I tried to hurry up before the car got too close to us, but it wouldn't stop. Next thing I knew, it was flashing lights.

I said, "I know this is not the police." We hurried and tried to pull our clothes back up, but it was too late. Two officers got out and told us to stay where we were. They poured out our beers and asked if we had any drugs on us which we didn't. Shannon told them that she was pregnant and wasn't drinking, so they told her to stay in the car. Then they asked if they could search us, and we said yes. One guy was on me and the other on Diana. They felt on us from top till bottom. Then they let us go with a warning. We were so happy they let us go. When we got in the car, Shannon said, "Y'all big dummies, those men wasn't supposed to search y'all. They supposed to call female officers over here to search y'all. Y'all can sue." I didn't remember their names; and at the time, I didn't care. I thought I was going to jail for indecent exposure or something. Throughout the years, Steve and Diana had another daughter and named her Starr, and the relationship wasn't getting any better. So Steve decided to move to West, Texas, and leave Diana.

A year later, I haven't come on my cycle, so I made an appointment to the doctor's office. Momma went with me. She told me, "You better not be pregnant. And if you are, I'm going to get a hanger and get it out myself." When I went in, they saw me back while momma waited in the waiting room. When I came out, I just looked at her and nodded my head. She said, "I know you're not pregnant," real loud.

And I told her, "Yes, I am." She just got up and walked out the doctor's office and went to her car. The nurse was standing right next to me and witnessed all this drama, so she asked if I was okay, needed a ride, or did I want to call someone. I told her no, that she was just being a drama queen.

When I got in the car, she was mad. She asked me, "How you going to take care of another baby? You barely taking care of the ones you got." I knew she was right, but it's done. So I tried my best to light up to mood.

I told her, "Because they have the best grandma in the world."

Momma loved all her grandkids, but she had a bond with De'vonte 'cause she helped raise him while I was still in school. She had him spoiled. He had her heart. She got him a PlayStation, Xbox, the latest shoes. Anything he wanted, she got it for him. I knew that if I needed her, she was going to be right there. I knew I was making mistakes, and she was just trying to help me not make the same mistakes she made.

Chapter 13

Months passed, and I had a beautiful baby boy named De'monyea. He was dark and very handsome, looks like a little man with silky black hair. I call him my little chocolate drop. After having him, I decided to get my tubes tied. Three kids is enough for me, plus I'm too young to be having all these babies with no daddy. De'monyea's daddy would help me if I needed anything, but he didn't want anything to do with him. He didn't want his old lady to know he had another child on her. They were living in separate houses, but they were still talking. When I made it home from having my baby, I was so sore from getting my tubes tied. I barely could walk to the restroom because the pain was so unbearable. I was grateful I had my mom, and he was a good baby.

I wonder why I always find myself with these nothing, no-good men. Maybe it's because the way my dad did my mom, or maybe I party too much for someone to take me seriously. The ones I tried to take seriously and be faithful and loyal would be the worst. I had my share of worthless men in my life. I have been abused and cheated on. This one guy I was dating, I was scared of him. He was very demanding, controlling, and insecure. He was on drugs, and I never knew what kind of mood he would be in. I kept the house clean, cooked, and worked, but he wasn't ever satisfied. One day, I didn't have a car at the time, so I walked to the store to get grocery. On the way, walking back home with two sacks full of groceries, I saw of Steve's friend, and he picked me up. When I made it to the house, my boyfriend was standing at the front door. So I got out of the car with the groceries, and he just looked at me, didn't try to help. When I made it into the house, he slapped me right in the mouth, food with everywhere. He accused me of going with guy that gave me a ride home.

When I be in these situations with these men, I know that I can do better. I just allowed myself to stay and put up with everything that I know is wrong. I just feel stuck and can't get out of it. I asked myself, *Why do I let myself go through this after seeing my parents in my whole childhood.* All I knew is I'm going to beg no man to be a father. A year passed. I wasn't going out every weekend like I used to, but I would still go every now and then. It's been a while since I have been out, and the girls and I decided to go. I had my all-over-body suit on, looking good, trying to see if I still got it. We went out to the club about seven miles away and having a good time. I have an overactive bladder, especially when I drink. I was tired of asking the girls to come with me to the restroom. They got to enjoy themselves too. The ghetto bar we were at, the door didn't have a lock. When you have on a bodysuit, you got to pull down everything and your boobs and everything be exposed. I'm thinking, *I just going to run in and out without anyone trying to open the door*, 'cause I had no one to hold the door.

Soon as I got done, as I'm trying to wipe, the door came open. I yelled, "Someone in here." But it continued to open. As I looked up, I saw this guy, the same guy who was staring me down on the dance floor. I hurried and tried to pull my clothes up.

He grabbed my arms while holding the door with his foot, telling me, "You know you want it," trying to kiss me. I'm trying to fight him off and pulling my clothes up at the same time.

I told him "I don't know you, and you think I'm going to give you some in this dirty restroom." We struggled for about five minutes, and I finally got my clothes up. And someone was knocking on the door. He gave up and left. I looked at myself in the mirror, and I had this fright, scared look on my face, and I started crying. I wiped my face and went out to get my girls and told them I was ready to go. When I step out of the restroom, I saw Rod. He's one of Steve and my good friend. He was standing right there by the restroom with a shocked look on his face, his mouth was wide open.

When I made it home, Rod called me and asked why I ran out the bar so fast. I was thinking, *Is he serious?* I knew he saw that dude come out the restroom 'cause he was standing right there. So I told him, "You saw that dude tried to rape me." I had so much emotions build up in me. I started crying. He said, "Wait, wait, I didn't know that that was you in the restroom. When I seen him coming out the lady's room, I thought he was in there with some trap. But when I seen you come out, it took me back a little, but I'm sorry I didn't know. Why you didn't say anything?"

I told him, "Just leave it alone. The dude didn't do anything. I stopped it before anything happened." It made me feel real good to know how concern he was. Ever since then, we have been close. He's like a brother to me that I always can come and talk to him about anything.

Chapter 14

A year later, I lost my job at the nursing home. So my older brother Adam suggested that we go to our home town in West, Texas, and sell dope. Now in West, Texas, you can sell your dope smaller and make as twice as much as you can in Calvert. At first, I was scared because I never sold any dope, and I knew the repercussion. I have never been to jail and wasn't planning on it either. I wanted to be a good example for my kids, and I sure didn't want them to grow up, thinking it was okay to sell drugs. I figured I will do this just once and don't get caught, save up a little money, and everything will be okay. I was convinced when I saw all the money he was bringing home. He would go down there for just the weekends and come back home stacked. All that money in just two days, I was ready to go in and out and have enough money to be on my feet. Selling dope was easy. My brother would cut up the dope for me in twenties, so all I had to do was give them what they wanted. If they wanted forty, then give them two and so on. Now I know why the boys on the corner be on the corner every day. This was easy money. We stayed out there in the weekend and come back home that Sunday. When I made it back home, Mommy was excited to see all the money that I made. She said, "You made this in two days." So she said next time we go back, she wanted to ride.

Mommy had Nita working home health for her, but she said Nita was lazy and didn't do anything but come to here and fall asleep on the couch. I told her she was pregnant and gave her a pregnancy test, and it came back positive. She was in denial. So she called her boyfriend Frank. He brought her a test, and it came back the same. He was still in denial, so he found the most expensive one he could find. He said if this comes back the same, then I'll believe it, and it came back positive. When she went to the doctor, they gave her a due date in April, close to De'monyea's birthday. So she didn't work for Momma anymore, and Momma was happy because she wanted to go with us when we went to West, Texas, next weekend.

So the next weekend, Adam, Mom, my kids, and I went out to West, Texas. My mom hasn't been back here ever since her husband died even though she said she was never coming back here, and it's probably brought up a lot of bad memories. But she was happy to come back because she had friends and family here. She wasn't selling dope; but when it comes to money, she wanted her cut. We made more money than last week. My mom visited all her old friends, her and the kids stayed in the room most of the time. When we made it back home, I bought a white Lincoln, and my mom got her a grey one. After buying the cars, our money got short, so we decided to go back. I know I said it was just a one-time thing; but once you see all that money and how easy it was to sell, you get addicted.

That summer back at home, it was very hot and nothing to do in Calvert, so I decided to take the kids to the lake. Every summer, I tried to do little family things together, and they love the water. Tina, Nita, and Tracy and their kids met Mark (Sue's son),the kids, and I there. Diana, Shannon, and their kids came also. The lake we went to had a section for swimming only. No boats or fishing on this side. The kids played in the water, and we would be right there in the water with our beer cans. De'monyea, my chocolate drop was three years old, and he was scared to get in the water which I didn't mind 'cause I didn't want him in there anyways. I didn't want him to drown. De'monyea couldn't talk yet, but he would say a few words. My other kids talked before their second birthday. He was just slow in talking; but he was smart because you tell him to do something, he will do it right away. But I didn't have to worry about him in the lake. The closest he would come is right by the shore and play in the sand.

The other kids knew that if the water pass your chest, then you are too far and need to turn around. I had this float I was floating on, so I went to go get De'monyea so he can get in the water too. We both was on this one float. As I'm on the float, I looked up into the sky and it was so beautiful. It felt like I was floating in heaven. I looked back at the kids playing in the water, and it was if they were playing in slow motion. This was a perfect moment. As I was daydreaming, I didn't realize we were floating too far to the deep side of the lake. I can swim but not that good. I got scared thinking, *If I get off this float I will turn it over and drown my baby.* I started to panic and thinking, *If I kill my baby, I don't know what I will do.* So I started screaming, "HELP, HELP." Diana's son, who was about fourteen at the time, pulled us back. I was so scared. I don't think my baby knew the danger he was in. After that, I made sure he didn't get in the water. The kids had a good time, and it was beautiful seeing the sun glazing down on the water. It really was amazing.

Chapter 15

The next weekend, we brought Sue and her son Mark, who is eighteen, back to West, Texas, with us. We all were selling why not let them get a piece of the action. My mom and the kids would be in a hotel room. While we set up at a friend's house, we would buy beer and drink like we were having an outdoor party. The whole time, the dope smokers would come in and out like they were partying but buying dope. Every Friday, they would be waiting on us to come to town. They said our dope was better than what they had. It was more potent. So when we came to town. We had a lot of dope. That's why we are all was selling and having fun doing it at the same time. It was like a family reunion. We already had family here, and Steve was just thirty miles away. The next day, we rented the VFW building, and all my family came. We barbequed, and all the kids ran around playing. We played dominos and Mingo around. Later on that evening, we all came inside. Greg DJed, and we all danced. It was nice, nothing but family, and no one was fighting. De'vonte got on the dance floor and had the crowd cheering, I didn't know he could dance that good. He loved watching dance movies and Chris Brown, and he really got some moves. I was so proud of him I said to myself, *Look at my baby. He's going to be a superstar.*

That following month school started back, so we had to stop on our trip to West, Texas. De'vonte was doing good in school. He was behind, but now he's paying more attention. And his grades are going up. He's into basketball and very excited about that. His team won the championship, and he got a trophy for the most valuable player. I was very proud of him and De'venna. De'venna is a very smart girl to be so young. She always made *A*s and only in the second grade, and De'monyea is starting to talk a little more. When we go to bed at night, he sleeps with me, and his little feet be so cold. So I tuck them in between my lower thigh so they could warm up. He got used to that; and one night, I forgot. He jammed his feet between my legs, and I laughed to myself. That's a thing we had to do every night. I said to myself I have good respectful kids, and they are getting older. I know I have to stop selling if I want to be a good example for them.

That weekend, I didn't go to West, Texas. I decided to stay and go out in Calvert. I put on my tight dress, the one that hugs my curves, and my makeup. I took the kids over Momma's house, so she could babysit. When I got to her house, she was sitting on the couch, watching TV. She asked me to get her medicine out the restroom. As I'm walking in the restroom, this funny feeling came across me. I told her, "It feels like something bad is going to happen."

She asked me, "What are you talking about?

I told her that I couldn't explain, but it just felt like something wasn't right.

She told me, "If you feel like something bad is going to happen, then maybe you need to stay at home tonight." So I didn't go out. Instead I stayed with my mom and watched movies all night. But that was the weirdest thing I ever felt. It was as if something was trying to warn me.

The next night, I went out with Mark. I bought some beer, and we just sat in the parking lot at the cafe. I was in my Lincoln, and he was in his car that he bought in West, Texas. After the bar closed, we weren't ready to go home, so Mark decided to race with our cars to see which one was the fastest. He was always bragging that his car was faster, so I wanted him to eat his words 'cause I know my car is faster. So we went on a road where there were no traffic, and I was in the left lame (coming to ongoing traffic), and he was in the right lame. We started, and I was winning. Then my car started smoking. I thought I had blew the heads, but the rear airbags deflated. And my shocks went out. So I had to park it, and let Mark have his shine. He really thought his car did something too.

The next weekend, we all were back to West, Texas. Momma decided to go since it was the weekend, and we'll be back before school starts on Monday. That Friday, we set up at the friend's house like always and stayed up all night drinking. The next day, I got up late, so I finally got up and ready to set up. Adam and Mark were already there, Adam told me the early bird gets the worms. I didn't care. I knew the smokers were going to come all day and night, so it didn't make a difference when I came. Before I made it to the friend's house, I saw cop cars. They had the whole corner blocked off. I was so scared. I just kept on going because I had dope on me. So I hurried up and put the dope inside of me just in case I get stopped. Then I rushed to the motel to check on my mom and the kids. When I got there, the laws were already there. They searched the room and were asking my mom and I about Steve, where he was and was he selling dope too. They finally let us go after harassing us for an hour.

We learned that they locked Adam up. They found dope on him, but they let Mark go. Adam took the blame and said that it was all his dope. I was so scared. That was too close. I have never been in jail, and I sure didn't want to go for selling dope. This was just supposed to be a one-time thing that went too far. We all packed and headed back home. Steve and his daughter Starr, who is four, came back with us. He had her all summer and was trying to put her in school in West, Texas. But he had to come back to Calvert to go to child support court in Bryan. We must fly back to Calvert. All I knew is I wasn't going to try to sell nothing—never again, not even a piece of gum. They gave Adam a bond, and we got him out the next day. My mom sent money to our cousin to get him out, and his wife and daughter brought him back home.

So all of us were back in Calvert; and every time Steve comes back home, we party all day and night. Everyone was at Momma's house (Sue, Mark, Sue's daughter Dee, Shannon and her kids, Adman and his daughter, and friends from the neighborhood). The kids played in the yard while De'vonte and Jim, Steve's oldest son, played video games in the house. Momma kept Jim a lot too since Steve was in West, Texas. She wanted him to be close to the family. Plus she loves her grandchildren. We ended the party early 'cause Steve had to go to court, and I had to be at the car lot. The next day, I got up early in the morning. I was excited to trade my Lincoln in for this newer Cadillac that they had. My Lincoln dropped about a week ago when Mark and I were racing, and it wasn't drivable. So they said I could come in today and trade it in, and they had this beautiful Cadillac that I want.

While I'm getting the kids ready for school, my mom was telling me that since De'vonte was doing good in school, she was going to take him to Bryan and get him a new video game after school. I said to myself, *She got him so spoiled.* Then I told her okay and that I was leaving shortly 'cause I didn't know how long I was going to be in Marlin, Texas. The kids left for school, and I started getting ready to go get my car. Steve's daughter was sleep, and my mom left to go to the nursing home to get her brother. He stayed in Calvert all his life 'cause they grew up on a farm on the outside of Calvert, and he never left. I think he's the reason why we moved to Calvert so she could be closer to him. He had a stroke years back and was paralyzed on one side; and the older he got, the more he needed help with everyday task. So he decided he wanted to go to a nursing home. When they came back, I tried to help her push the wheelchair in the house, and she was acting mad, pushing my hand out the way and wasn't saying anything when I tried to talk with her. I'm thinking, *What's her problem?* She did have mood swings. I said to myself, *Let me get the hell out of here 'cause I'm in a good mood. Going to get my car and nothing going to spoil my mood today.* So I dropped De'monyea, my baby, with the neighbor. She loves children. And he loves going over there because she was keeping another boy his age, and he loves to play with him.

Chapter 16

When I got my Cadillac, I was so excited. It's marble green and a newer model than my Lincoln; and when I hit the highway, it felt like I was flying or floating 'cause it drives so smooth. It's almost perfect. I just need music, and I know just the person to call, Steve. I might as well put him to work before he goes back home. I called him and asked if he would put my stereo and speaker in for me. He said yes and told me he was at Greg's house. I had to pass through Calvert first to go to Bryan. When I made it to Calvert, it was about 3:00 PM, and the kids were just getting out of school. I would take them to school in the mornings; but after school, they would walk depending on the weather. So they were walking home, and I passed right by them. They didn't know who I was. I stopped and they saw it was me. They both were excited to see my new car. De'vonte said, "Ohhh, this your car."

I said, "Yeah, do you like it?" They got in, and we rode a few blocks. Then I dropped them off at Momma's house. I didn't get out because I was in a hurry to get my music hooked up, and Momma had an attitude with me early this morning.

I pulled in Greg's yard, and Steve came right out and started on my car. I told my homegirl Chris, a friend from Calvert that rode to Bryan with me, to walk with me to the store so I could get something to eat. The store was just around the corner from Greg's house, and they made the best burgers in town. So Chris and I left walking. It was going to take Steve a while to hook my music up, so I had plenty of time. We made it to the store. It took them about thirty minutes to make the food. When we were headed back to Greg's, I saw Steve walking toward us. I looked at Chris and asked, "Why is he walking this way for? He knew we were going to the store. If he wanted something back, he should've just asked, and I would've brought it back". But when I got closer to him, I saw the panic in his eyes. I asked, "What's wrong?" He said one of his friends just called and said it was a bad wreck on highway 6 and that it looks like Momma's Lincoln.

As we were walking back to the car, the same friend called back and said that he didn't know if it was momma's car; but whoever's car it was, there were no survivors.

The moment he said that, my heart started racing uncontrollably. I started shaking at the same time trying to remain calm. We all rushed in the Cadillac, and I started driving going down highway 6. I'm thinking to myself, *I got to know if it's Momma's car, and I got to know now*. I started speeding going about 110 down the highway. I could hear Chris telling Steve, "Please tell her to slow down."

He said, "Syrup, slow down. We don't know if it's even Momma, and we don't want to have a wreck ourselves.

Now I'm praying, "Please don't let it be Momma. Please don't let it be Momma, please." The cars on the highway were at a stop about ten miles or more from the wreck scene, and we couldn't see anything but a line of cars built up. So I drove on the opposite side of the highway. Cars weren't going from either sides, and I saw the ambulance. I got as close as I could. Ambulances and police were everywhere. We tried to walk up closer, but a cop stopped us and said we couldn't come any closer. I couldn't really tell if it was Momma's car because it was wrecked so bad. But I saw two bodies lying in the road with sheets over them. They were about twenty feet apart, and there's a sheet over the driver too.

Chapter 17

A state trooper came over and gave Steve Momma's driving license, and I just broke down in tears. He told him that it was her and four kids, three died and one survived. He said we can later identify them; but right now, they were still investigating. He said he believed momma clipped the front of the eighteen-wheeler as both were traveling south. She spun out, and all the kids were ejected at least fifteen to twenty feet. Another car traveling northbound hit her again. He said that this was the worst accident ever seen 'cause of not wearing seatbelts. I broke down, Steve trying to hold me. All I saw was two bodies lying in the road, and I know the driver has to be momma. But there was another body on the other side of the car that we couldn't see on the side we were standing. We didn't know who exactly the kids were. Steve's daughter was here. And Momma kept his son Jim all the time and De'monyea was with the neighbor. We just didn't know, and it was the worst feeling in the world. Then I saw De'venna's dad in the crowd; and he came up to us and said he saw De'venna. They had to air fly her in the helicopter to a children's hospital.

It was so many people out here. There was a large group on the south and north side of the scene. We stayed out there for hours. Now I'm in shock. Everything seemed like a big bad dream. It feels as if I'm high or something, everything just blurry. They finally got the road cleared; and as we were leaving, I saw my brother Adam out there. I looked him right in his eyes, and he looked just as helpless as me. He is more like the father figure 'cause he was way older, but this was something we couldn't control or do anything about. Before we left, a state trooper came back and tried to describe the age and sizes of the children the best he could for his reports so we could identify them. He said it was a boy between ten or twelve. And I knew it right away that it was De'vonte because him and Jim were the same age, but he was much bigger than Jim. If you didn't know him, you would think he was older, plus Momma wasn't going anywhere without taking him. Then I remembered Momma saying she was going to take him to get a game for doing good in school. Then he said a young girl about four or five; and we knew it was Starr, Steve's baby girl. Then he said an infant about two or three, and I said, crying, "That's my baby." I thought De'monyea was still with the neighbor, and my mom hardly ever take him with her.

I just can't believe this has happened. I lost my two boys, mom, and niece all at one time, and who knows what kind of condition my baby girl is in. My mind went blank. I couldn't even think someone drove me home. I can't remember. I was still in shock. I remember being at the house, looking through the closet, trying to find some clothes so I can go to Temple Texas, to the hospital with De'venna. As I'm looking for clothes, a pair of De'monyea's shoes fell from the top of the closet right in front of me. I started crying again saying, "My baby, my baby, gone." I broke down again, and one of my good friend Trika picked me up. Trika drove me to the hospital because I was in no way, in shape or form, able to drive. When I made it to the hospital, my brother Greg was already there. He has always been this calm, relax person, and he was trying his best to be calm. But I could see the spook in his eyes too. He told me that De'venna was in surgery and that they were putting a plate in her hip because she has a broken hip. She has a broken hip, a fractured femur bone (which the doctors say she might not have any children in the future), and a few cracked ribs.

When they rolled her to her room, she was asleep, I guess from the medicine they gave her for surgery. I walked up to her bed and started crying again. Her face was all scratched up from the pavement of the road, and her lip was busted. I'm thinking, *She has been through so much just to be six years old*. There was this priest walking around the hospital, and the nurse asked if I wanted him to come in and pray. I told her that I didn't want him in the room right now for praying. I just want De'venna to rest. I'm thinking to myself, *What kind of God takes away little children*, and was very angry with God. He should've took me instead of my kids. I'm the one with all the sin. Those kids were still babies and had a whole future ahead of them. How can something like this happen so fast. I don't understand, and I hate God for ruining my life. I just got to concentrate on not losing my only child I have left and give all my attention to her. De'venna stayed asleep all that evening. I couldn't sleep. I just cried silently. I didn't want to wake her up. I was not sure if she was aware of what just happened and if she will remember anything when she wakes up. She woke up in the middle of the night screaming, and that really hurt me more to see her go through all this pain and can't do anything about it but just watch.

Chapter 18

The next day Nita called me, and I said "Hello."

And she said, "Hello." That was the only thing that was said. We just held the phone in silence for about twenty minutes, in mute. She knew that there were no words that would make me feel better, but I felt her sympathy. Ray and Dee came to visit. I was happy to see them because there was so much going on. I didn't think anyone would be able to visit. De'venna was up and talking. We didn't say anything about the wreck to her. The doctor still had her on some pain medicine. She was in and out. They stayed most of the evening, but they had to go back home before it got dark. That night, the same thing happened. She woke up screaming. It was a hard night for the both of us. The next day, I got a phone call from this lady. I didn't recognize her voice. She told me she was a paramedic who was on the scene. She said she saw me on the highway, and she felt so bad for me and wanted to give her condolence. She also asked how De'venna was doing and that she was praying for the both of us. I really appreciated her taking the time out of her day, being concern about people she didn't know. That gave me a little hope. I didn't get her name, but it meant a lot to me.

Steve called me and told me I need to come back home so we can make funeral arrangements. But first, I had to talk with De'venna and ask her if she remembered anything and if she knows why she was in the hospital. She said that she didn't remember anything. I asked her, "Do you remember getting in the car with your grandma and brothers and cousin?" She said she remembered getting in the car; but after that, she didn't remember. She said when she got into the car, she fell asleep. I told her what happened and that everyone that was in the car except her died. She just cried. We both cried together. I hugged her so tight. My sister Queen came and stayed at the hospital with De'venna while I went back to Calvert. Queen was with her husband. She didn't have any children, but she loved mine like there were her own.

She said, "We all hurting from this tragedy, and I know you have to go. But I can't see anyone else with De'venna but me." And I agreed.

As we got to the funeral home, it all seemed so unreal, but reality snapped me back in my place. Here I am, picking out caskets for my boys. Never in my life would I imagine this would be happening. My brother Steve and I always had a bond because we were so close in age, but I didn't want to share losing a child with him. No parent should bury their child. He made me strong 'cause he seemed to be holding on pretty good. Steve used to work at the funeral home before he moved to West, Texas. That's why we picked that particular one. They told us that our mom was messed up too bad, so she would have to have a closed casket. We picked her out a white casket. Diana and Steve picked out a pink casket for Starr. I wanted my boys to be buried together, so I had to order a plus-size casket which was sky blue. We decided to have their funeral in Calvert and bury them in West, Texas, because that's where our family were buried at. Momma had insurance, and she had De'vonte on a plan as well. But De'monyea and Starr wasn't on insurance. So the funeral director suggested we delay the funeral another week to give us enough time to raise more money to bury them, and we agreed.

We had to write out the obituary and agree on what we want in it. De'monyea's father work at the funeral home, and he was there when we were writing up the obituary. The funeral director asked about the fathers. I put Joe's name down as De'vonte's father. Then he asked me about the youngest, and I said his father's right here. Then De'monyea's father looked at me with this crazy look and said "I don't want my name on there. I don't want my old lady to know I had another child on her."

I started crying and I told him, "Your son is dead, and you going to deny him." I could not understand. I'm going through all this, and he's adding more fuel to the fire. I got up and slapped the taste out of his mouth before I realized what I was doing. Steve grabbed me and told me to leave it alone. If he don't want his name on there, just let it be. It still hurt me. I knew he had a girlfriend, but they were separated and lived in two different house. My baby and his dad looked like twins. I just couldn't believe he is denying him. We gave them all the picture we wanted in the obituary. Each family member wrote a little poem or message that we put in there. Steve put in his "it hurt me so much because Starr looked so much like Momma. Now I lost both at the same time. Where do I go from here."

They told us to bring them back clothes—everything from socks, underwear, shoes, and whatever we wanted them to be buried in. I got upset all over again because I remember Momma telling me that when she dies, she wanted to be buried in her white dress in the closet, and she wanted me to do her hair. I can hear her saying, "Don't be scared to do my hair. I don't want anyone else in my head. You do my hair." I'm thinking, *How can I do her hair when she has a close casket.* I asked the funeral director if I could, and he said it was no way possible. She was messed up too bad. She also told me she wanted to be buried with Al. She already had a plot at the military cemetery but that wasn't going to happen now because she took her grandkids with her, and I didn't want them to be buried alone. She always took De'vonte with her everywhere she went, and she took him in death too. It is all just so surprising and unexpected.

You hear people say all the time, "When they lose a child or a close family member, that a part of them dies too." That is so true. I feel so empty like I have been raped or something. A part of my heart is missing, and I don't think it will ever come back. It's hard to explain.

We headed to Bryan, Texas to buy them their clothing to be buried in. I picked out my boys some white tuxedos and white shoes. Diana picked out Starr this beautiful gold dress. Then we went to get their underwear and socks. When I walked into the store, I felt as if everyone was staring at me. It could've been my imagination, but it sure felt like it. As I'm picking out underwear, I started crying thinking this is the last time ever that I get to buy them underwear. My baby boy was only three. He was still wearing pull-ups, so this was the first and the last time buying him underwear. I was an emotional wreck. We found everything and took it back to the funeral home. Now all we have to do is go home and get Momma's dress. On the way back home, I tried to gather myself. I looked at the other cars passing by. Then I saw one of Jeff's daughter, and she looked at us and started shaking her head and crying as we passed her up. I was thinking a lot of people are hurting, and I knew her and momma were close even after Jeff and her broke up.

When we got to Calvert, I couldn't believe how everyone was so supportive. This was my first time being back since the wreck. It's such a small town. Everyone knows everyone, and they all knew about the wreck. All day I heard "sorry for your loss," and "if you need anything, let me know." Steve told me that he talk to De'venna's dad and that he told him he would come to the hospital while we handled our funeral arrangements. But he had to get Queen to come 'cause at the last minute, he didn't want to come. Steve and De'venna's dad were classmates, and another one of their classmates Jay heard that he wouldn't come to the hospital. Jay was mad and beat him up.

He told Steve, "You all going through all this. He could've got off his sorry butt and be with his daughter while y'all take care of business." I was grateful that he did that 'cause it was true. I didn't need him to come. He had never done anything for her before. Different people brought food to the house. Nita's mom came over and cleaned for us. I just felt the love, and everyone sympathized with us. The news camera came, and Jim got on there—only ten years old, talking and crying about how he's going to miss them all. He told me since De'venna lost her brothers that he was going to be her big brother from now on. He was so young, and I know he didn't know how much that really meant to me.

CHAPTER 19

A couple days later, the hospital released De'venna. It was a bittersweet moment. I was happy she was coming home yet sad at the same time. When we made it to Calvert, the high schools were having their homecoming parade, so I asked her if she wanted to go. She has been in that hospital for almost two weeks, and it would be nice to get out and get some fresh air. So we went up town, and I got the wheelchair out the back and put her in it and rolled her in front of the crowd so she could see the parade. The parade was so nice, and De'venna was really enjoying herself. Then I looked, and there was De'vonte's picture on one of the floats. His classmates did it in memory for him. I thought, *That was sweet of them.* But some kids can be cruel sometimes. I didn't cover De'venna up enough; and some little boy said, "De'venna, wearing a diaper." It hurt her feelings, and she was ready to go home. I was ready to go anyways. I knew we have a big day ahead of us; and tomorrow is the day of the wake, then Saturday, the day of the funeral. I know that's going to drain all the life out of me, so I need all the rest I can get, which I doubt but I'm going to try.

The day of the wake, it was so many people that came—all my siblings, aunts, uncles, nieces, nephews, cousins and lots of friends, from momma friends to one of the sibling's friends, down to De'vonte's friends. It was so emotional seeing my boys lying in that casket. They looked so handsome; and I thought to myself, *At least they were together.* I examined their bodies. They looked just like themselves, as if they were sleeping. You had to be right on them to notice anything different, but I could tell because I was inspecting everything. When you're not there when it happens, you want to know what happened, who hit who, how did they fly out the car, did they suffer. These were questions I had that no one could answer. We were all just clueless. Nobody in the family knew nothing, just what the trooper told us; and he was only going by what the truck driver told him. It could've been his or Momma's fault, who knows.

When you first walk to their casket, you see De'monyea. He was in the front or left side and De'vonte on the right side of him. De'monyea has little scratches on his face, but you could barely see it with all the makeup they have on him. De'vonte looked just like himself, not a scratch on him; but if you look on his right side, there was this big knot on the side of his head. It wasn't noticeable because the way he was lying in the casket, and the casket door was blocking his right side. But I wanted to see everything. I'm thinking, *That's probably the blow that killed him.* I'm just trying to put all this together and just can't figure it out. I didn't know what to feel. A minute I'm sad, mad, and then just hopeless. I was mad at Tina months ago, before the accident; but when I saw her come in the wake with tears in her eyes, I just embraced her. Life's too short to be fighting over little things, and I know she loves me and feel the pain with me.

After the awake ended, I told my siblings I need to get drunk. Today was hard, and I know tomorrow is even harder with the actual funeral. So we all decided to go out. Nita's mom watched De'venna. I trusted her. She used to babysit for me all the time, and I knew she wasn't going to let nothing happen to her. As I'm walking into the bar, I saw Tracy. This was the first time seeing her since the accident; and when she saw me, she grabbed me and hugged me. I started crying. She held me so tight. My knees gave out and I hit the ground. I bald up on the ground crying. Then Steve came and picked me up and told Tracy to give me some space. He said he wasn't trying to be rude; but every time someone comes up to me, I break down. Shannon calmed me down. Then we went inside the bar because I really needed a drink. So we went inside the bar. Most of the people in the bar were my family member. Shannon and I were sitting at this little table by the bar, and we got our drinks. It kind of eased my mind a little.

After a couple of drinks, the atmosphere changed. My oldest brother Mike and Sue were telling Adam and Steve that "We're the oldest and we want to see Momma." They were demanding to see her. They said, "We don't care how bad she is. We can handle it. Before we have their funeral tomorrow, we can see her." Shannon and I were just looking, but we all wanted to see her. So I wanted to know how far will this go. The next thing I know Adam pushed Mike, and Steve was trying to hold him back.

Adam was fighting mad. He said, "We all want to see Momma. If we could, we would. They wouldn't let Steve see her, and he used to work there. So just leave it alone". The whole bar was a mess. Tables and chairs were everywhere. It all happened so fast I was confused. We all were hurting, but this is the wrong way to do things. Instead of arguing, we need to be together for one another.

Chapter 20

Today is the funeral day, the day I dread. I just can't let go. I was not ready to say goodbye, and I know this was the last day I will ever get to see my boys. I thought this whole time that Momma would die older in the hospital. I have been taking her to the hospital back and forward due to her diabetes ever since I was a teenager. Never would've I thought I would be burying her with my kids. Then the guilt started to kick in. And I thought, *What if I would have drove Momma to Bryan that day, maybe they would still be alive. I was going there anyway. I could've drove them.* All this guilt and what if's kept coming up, and it made me sad because it made me feel like I could have done something to save them. I pushed all that aside and started getting ready for the funeral.

Everyone came. There were so many people. The family took up one side of the church, and the siblings sat in the first two rows. I'm thinking, *This is the first time all eight of us were together in one place.* Dee pushed De'venna in. We all looked nice in our black. It's sad that it took something like this to happen to bring all of us together.

There were so many people that most of them had to stand outside, even the news camera were there. I thought, *That was odd* but no energy to argue with anyone. It's like I'm having a bad dream and can't wake up. But it's all coming to realization, especially when they opened the caskets. I looked across from me and saw De'vonte's classmates. They were all sitting together. It sure did hurt me to see all those kids crying and hurting. Then I imagined De'vonte sitting right with them. Then I started thinking, *Why this happen? Why are my babies lying in that casket now?* I just didn't understand. The funeral home did a nice job. Everything was so beautiful and organized, perfect. They had Momma in the far left; and in front of her casket, there was a picture of her when she was younger. Starr was in the middle. Her little pink casket was so small. I have never seen a child casket before other than on TV, but not in real life. My boys were on the other end. As the people walked by to view their bodies, they were crying. That made me cry. I was not trying to cry because I wanted to be strong for De'venna. Then she started crying, and Dee took her out. And I just broke down.

When it was my time to view their bodies, I went to Momma first and touched her casket, wishing I could see her one last time to say my proper goodbye. My mother was a strong woman, the stick to the glue that held our family together. Now it's all gone in a flick of moment. While I'm touching her casket, I'm thinking, *Momma, what happened?* I just wanted to know what went wrong that day. Then I went to Starr's casket. My little niece was so beautiful. I can just hear her voice. "Aunt Syrup, Aunt Syrup." Then I viewed my boys. I stared at them for a long time, touching their little cold hands, knowing this will be the last time I get to touch them. After the funeral, the family met at the funeral home to decide who's going to ride with who to our trip to West, Texas, for the burial. The funeral director left in the middle of our meeting. I'm thinking, *Maybe he went to gas up the hearse.* But he came with a trash bag in his hand. He whispered something in one of his worker's ears, and they went to the back.

So we left and made it to West, Texas. Our family and friends that couldn't come to the funeral came to the burial. It was stressful because it was like doing it all over again, but we didn't open the caskets which the people out there wanted us to do. The funeral director told the men who did their grave to not open the casket and wait until we all left before they put them into the ground. We just passed out obituaries, said a prayer, and put them in the ground. We stayed all night in West, Texas, and went to a cousin's house where they barbecued for us. Steve and Diana were trying to work things out and get back together. Before Starr died. She wanted her mom and dad together again, and they tried to do it for her. But that didn't last very long. Steve thinks Diana blames Momma for Starr's death, and things were just complicated. Things just happen that we can't explain, but she knows Momma wouldn't do anything to hurt those kids intentionally. When we made it back to Calvert, there was a rumor going around in town that Momma's head was cut off and that she was buried without it.

We were all concerned about this rumor, and everyone was asking us if it was true, and this was the first time we had heard it. So Steve went to go ask the funeral director because he used to work for him; and if anybody can get an answer, he knew he could. The allegations were true. He told him he didn't wanted to tell us because we've been through so much and that her head was found. He also said her head was found, and it was buried with her body. He basically blamed everything on the police. But Steve asked why wasn't anyone told, and he really couldn't explain. He just guaranteed that her whole body was in the ground. We were all hurting all over again. We didn't know that she was decapitated. We were told that the seatbelt did it. That's why the police were at the scene so long. They were looking and couldn't find it. De'monyea's dad was the one who told everyone in Calvert about it. He knew because he works at that funeral home. He was telling them not to say anything to the family about it. Everyone knows how gossip get out, and everyone was talking and adding on their parts that it was bound to come back to us. I was already mad at him for denying my baby, but this takes the cake. He could've came to either one of us and told us instead of gossiping to everyone in town. We also learned that there were mowers working on the side of the road that found her head.

Chapter 21

Two days later, I took Sue back to the funeral home. We were hurting, and we had questions. She was crying, telling the funeral director that they could've told someone in the family and how did we know if her whole body was in the grave. "You lied this whole. How do I know you not lying now?" He told her that the day we left to bury them in West, Texas, is when they found her. Some mowers working on the highway found her, and it was turned in to another funeral home. Well, when we were in our meeting and he left in the middle of the meeting and came back with a bag, well, our mom's head was in that bag. We just cried knowing now this whole time. We had a wake and funeral, and her whole body wasn't in her casket. Most black people have their funeral in two weeks after they die. But what if we would have had it sooner? Were they not going to tell us? I'm just thinking and replaying it over and over, and I can hear my mom telling me she wanted me to do her hair. She wasn't even in there. Maybe that's why it stayed on my mind. She was trying to tell me. How can the laws leave the scene like that. It's not a finger or a toe. It's a person's head. They should've informed someone in the family. Someone should have told us, and everyone in town knew about it but us.

Just imagine how the mowers felt when they were working and found something like that. I bet they were traumatized. What if they would've mowed over her? Then we surely would have been hurt, but we still don't really know if they were just honest at first. Then we would trust him more. He assured us that she was whole when they put her in the ground. He also told us that her head was in perfect condition, that it didn't have a scratch on it. I'm thinking, *Perfect condition, what does that mean? We could've had an open casket?* Sue started cursing him out and crying, telling him, "That's our mom. She shouldn't be treated like some trash on the street."

I grabbed her and told her, "Let go." We left there more confused than when we first came and emotionally tired. That night, we put out flowers and crosses on the side of the road where they died. All the family and friends that stayed close by were there. We lighted candles in their memory and said a prayer.

Two weeks later, De'venna has been in the house, and she wanted to go over to Nita's house to stay all night with her daughter. They get along so well, and no wheelchair was going to stop her. She's been taking steps to go to the restroom and been doing really good. So I let her stay, and Nita's daughter was happy to see her. The next day, I went to Nita's house to pick her up; and when I went inside, here's Nita picking her up, lifting her from the restroom. I looked at Nita and asked her, "What are you doing?"

She said, "What?"

I told her, "De'venna could have walked to the restroom. She does it at home." De'venna just started laughing.

Nita said, "Girl, I know you haven't had me picking your big butt to the restroom all night and day." We all started laughing.

She was healing up really fast. Her doctor didn't think she would be walking this soon. He said about six months, she would be walking; but when I took her for her monthly checkup, she was walking. She had a limp, but he was amazed to see her walking so soon. She's a strong little girl. She told me she didn't wanted to ride the handicap bus to school. She stated the kids would make fun of her. It's sad how kids can be sometimes. It makes me angry. But I know they don't understand everything she's been through, and it did motive her to walk early. I now know that she was ejected from the car like the other kids. A witness that was on the scene on the highway said that she was lying in the middle of the highway, crying for her momma before she was airlifted. There were some critics from the news website that talk bad about Momma. They couldn't understand how a grandma can put her grandkids in a car and not put them in seatbelts, and she had on one. But everything happens for a reason; and maybe if they were wearing seatbelts, I wouldn't be able to see them for the last time like momma.

My sadness became anger, almost rage I became mad at the truck driver. I didn't know him, and I didn't know who was at fault. But all I knew is that he took my family away. It was hard to watch or hear people talk about their kids; and I hate when strangers asked, "Do you have any kids? Or how many do you have?"

I always say, "Three but one now," and they want to know why. Sometimes I just don't want to explain. I was mad at God. My kids were innocent. They were too young, haven't live their life, and my baby was only three. What's the use of having a baby if he's just going to take them away so soon. Another lady said she was behind Momma that day. She said she didn't see what happened, who hit who cause it all happened so fast, but she saw the kids fly out the car. She said she was traumatized about that. She said that had affected her, and she was scared to drive with her children in the car.

I needed a break from Calvert, so I decided to move to Big Spring, Texas with Steve. It was just too overwhelming for me in Calvert, and I needed to get away before I go nuts. It was peaceful down there because everyone didn't know my history, and where we stayed was about thirty miles from where we grew up at. So I could easily go and visit their graves whenever I wanted to. I put De'venna in school and started working at the nursing home close by his house. I started missing my family and friends back in Calvert. So I moved back and stayed with Tina for a while and returned to my old job at the nursing home where my uncle was. Momma wasn't here anymore to take him out and get his personal things. But I made sure he was taken care of. Anything he needed. Six months later, he had another stroke and didn't make it. He died exactly one year and a day apart from Momma and the kids' death date.

I began to be in a deep depression. I was now drinking every day, and the drinking wasn't numbing my pain. It's feels like I'm just mourning. I tried to stay strong for so long now. I'm just breaking down. I thought of suicide, but how can I kill myself? I'm all De'venna got. If she would not have survived, I already know I would be dead by now. Mark is staying with me now, and he's helping me out. I didn't want them to see me cry. I was trying to be strong, especially in front of De'venna, but I knew Mark could see me breaking down. The holidays was the worst because we used to all get together and eat at Momma's house. Things just wasn't the same. The house seemed empty without her in the kitchen cooking and the kids playing and running around. We tried getting to together, but things didn't work out. Someone will be talking about the other, or it will be at two different houses. And we just stopped trying. Momma was the common source of the family. No matter what kind of difference we had with each other, she will make them right; and if she tells you you were coming to her house, then you were coming no matter how old you were. If she tells us something, we listen.

Chapter 22

Couple months later, that really worried Sue about the wreck, especially the way they did to us about our mom. She had a bump growing on her neck. At first, we thought it was a boil, but it never came to a head. One night, when I was doing her hair, she said, "Syrup, I don't think Momma is resting."

I asked her, "Why do you think that?" She said she doesn't know, but it was more that we should have done. We need to do something about it. Her story needs to be heard. I asked what should we do, and she said she didn't know. But she started writing every night. She would write in her tablet.

One day, I went to her house; and she said, "Syrup, look at this." And when I looked at her, I was shocked. I never seen anything like that before. That bump that was on her neck grew like a golf ball.

I told her, "You need to go to the doctor." She hates going to the doctor. You had to literally make her go. She was in good shape and moved around faster than all the young girls at work; but if she gets sick, she would lie in the bed for days without going to the doctor.

She was scared to go. She didn't want it to be nothing bad; but I told her, "You will never know unless you go to the doctor and see what is that hanging off your neck."

So she went to the doctor, and they did all kinds of test on her. It came back that she had cancer. When she came home and told Mark, Dee, and I the news, we all started crying. Sue smoked cigarettes ever since I knew her. Maybe that's what caused it. It's just another one of those things were you just don't know. I told her, "You can beat this. We will do whatever it takes to make this go away." They started her on chemo right away; and when she came home from chemotherapy, she became very sick. She didn't eat, and she would have these constant headaches. Her hair was slowly starting to come out. Before I knew it, she was bald.

She looked at me with tears in her eyes and said, "Syrup, all my hair gone."

I told her, "It's going to be okay." But truly I really didn't know. She lost so much weight. She looked like a skeleton. I felt so bad, and I wanted to be her biggest supporter. I shaved the side of my head so she would feel a little better about her appearance. One of her good friends she used to work with at the nursing home took her back and forward from the doctor's office; and every time she came home from chemo, she came back sick.

They scheduled an appointment for her to cut the tumor on the side of her neck. It was an hour away. We all thought it was a good idea, and I had hope and just knew they would get all the cancer out. So her kids and I went with her, and the operation came out good. After the surgery, she wanted to go stay with our sister Queen, who stayed close by the hospital where she had surgery. Queen said there were a lot of good doctors in her home town. So she went with Queen. She would call every day and asked about her grandkids. Dee just had her baby that she adores, and her other grandkids by her oldest son Ray. She sounded happy on the phone, and she said that Queen found her a good doctor. One day Queen call me and told me that Sue woke her up in the middle of the night. When she went into her room, there was blood everywhere. It came from when she had surgery on her neck. The stitches busted open. She told me it looked like somebody had sliced her neck wide open. So she rushed her to the hospital. It took them awhile to get the bleeding to stop, but they finally got it under control and sewed it back together. They told her that the cancer is spreading back.

She stayed with Queen for a couple months, but she was ready to come home. She missed her kids and grandkids. So I went to go pick her up, we were all so excited for her being back home. She stayed with her daughter Dee, who was right next door to us. I would help her in the daytime while Dee's at work, and she would help her at night time. She would have her good days and bad days. On her good days, we would ride around town anywhere she wanted to go; but on her bad days, she would lie in bed, crying in pain. I felt so helpless on those days because there was nothing that I could do about the pain just being there. One day, I went over to check on her, and she was dressed up with her makeup on and told me, "I'm ready to ride." She told me she wanted to go to the nursing home where she used to work. She liked visiting the patients, and they love her as well. I'm thought, *Here she is, sick but still have time for others.* After her visit, I took her home and I went to my house to get De'venna who was just getting out of school.

When I went back to Dee's house, Sue was in the kitchen frying up some fish. I said, "What are you doing? Let me do that."

She told me, "No, no, I got this." She made a big pan of fish, fried biscuits, and french fries she used to make all time before her sickness. She fixed her a big plate and sat down to eat. She took one bite and couldn't eat anymore.

Six months later, Sue's condition has gotten worse. The doctors suggested that we put her in a nursing home. But Dee and I wasn't going to let that happen. She worked at the nursing home; and she had seen when most young people goes into a nursing home, they lose their will to fight. So we agreed on hospice. That way, she can stay at home. The nurses would come to the house and do their visit. Every day I would go over there and sit and talk with her. She always likes talking about Momma and the kids a lot. She told me how Momma always had our backs. She told me this one time, she was coming from her boyfriend's house. She was riding down a street when someone shot at her and busted the back window out of her car. She was shaking and scared, so she went to Momma's house and told her, "Somebody trying to kill me." So her and Momma jumped in the car, and Momma had her gun with her. She told Sue to show her where she was when they shot at her. So Sue showed her, and they didn't see anyone but this old man mowing his yard. Momma looked in the back of her back seat and saw this rock and started laughing.

She told Sue, "Nobody was shooting at you. That old man that was mowing, must have ran over a rock that flew into the glass and broke the window." We both laughed, and she said Momma was right there if anyone of us needed her.

Chapter 23

A month later, Sue's cancer has taken over, and she wasn't eating and was in the bed all the time. She fought a good fight. But the cancer took over, and she passed. We buried her in West, Texas, right next to Momma and the boys. In her obituary, I wrote, "You take care of my kids in heaven, and I will take care of yours on earth." Sue was the oldest, and I looked up to her. She was more than a sister. She was my best friend, my everything. She was outspoken, say what she wanted to say. Everyone that met her, she had an impact on them. She was loved by everyone that knew her, and there were so many people at her funeral. I think she knew she was dying. That's why she wanted to come back home so she could spend time with her kids and grandkids before she died. It sure took her way to fast. I always thought she will overcome this disease. I never thought of death as an option. The little hope I had is now lost. We did everything together, worked, went out. She taught me everything about men and just life in general. I just couldn't believe all this has happened. Death seemed to be following me. I felt so delicate that at any moment I'm going to break in pieces. How much can one person take.

Couple days later, I was leaving the bar, walking home; and I saw a couple of guys on the corner, smoking wet. It's phencyclidine, PCP, or angel dust among other names. It's liquid form that you dip in a cigarette and smoke and it causes you to hallucinate and to be paranoid. I knew the consequences of smoking wet. This isn't weed. This was some hardcore drugs, and I saw how the guys would trip when they be on it, walking naked and looking like zombies. I was going through so much pain and emotions built up inside of me, things that I been holding back like Steve telling me that when the accident happened and someone said it was one survivor, he wish that it was his daughter. I knew he was hurting too, and he didn't want De'venna dead. It just hurt me. If I would've lost all my kids, I know I would've killed myself. I'm thinking to myself, *Maybe I should do it now I'm not living right. It's not his daughter but maybe he can take care of De'venna.* I was holding all this back in my mind; and at that moment, the wet sounded like a good idea. And alcohol just wasn't doing it.

So I asked one of the guys if can I hit their wet stick, and he gave it to me. As soon as I hit it, the high came all over my body. It was a good feeling. I felt like I could do anything like superman; and at that moment, the pain was gone. The next day, I went to find my friend Tracy. She smoked wet too, and we went to get high together. When we smoked, the both of us were in another world. We both were going through some things, and this was our medicine. It was a supernatural feeling. Sometime when I smoke, I could see my boys; and in a way, I felt I was closer to them. Wet was real easy to get. Every boy on the corner was selling some type of drug. Steve would send me money, and I would use that to get high. I felt bad because I could've done something else with the money, but I had a habit now, and every day I was smoking. It was shameful and embarrassing, but I just couldn't stop myself.

One night, Tracy and I were smoking, and Mark recorded us while we were tripping. I was sitting on the bed rocking back and forward holding my heart saying some words I couldn't understand. Tracy was in the back room, screaming. You could hear her yelling from the front of the room where I was, so Mark took the camera to the back room where she was. She was yelling and stomping the floor. When we came into, he showed us the video and how we were hallucinating. I couldn't remember anything; and if I didn't see it for myself, I wouldn't believe it. I felt shame and guilt all at once. I don't want to be walking around looking like a fool, and this drug has taken over me. I know I'm stronger than that. Plus I have De'venna who looks up to me. She wasn't there. She stayed a night over Nita's house. I would never smoke in front of her anyways, and I didn't want her to see me high and tripping.

One night, I was smoking, and I made it home. So I lay in my bed to go sleep. As I was lying in the bed, I saw this black dot floating above me, and it was moving closer and closer toward me. The closer it got to me, the bigger it became. As it got close to my face the, darkness went into my eyes and I couldn't see anymore. I didn't know if I was hallucinating, but it sure felt real. My high should've went down by now. I was lying in the bed blind. I started to panic after a few minutes when my sight didn't come back. I started praying, "Lord, please give me my eyesight back. I'm not going to smoke again." I laid in the bed about thirty minutes, totally scared to death. Then my sight came back, and I was thankful. The next day, I didn't tell anyone about that experience because I wasn't sure what actually happened, but it scared the hell out of me. I didn't smoke that day, but the temptation was calling me. I tried; but the next day, I had to go find me something to smoke.

Chapter 24

My dad, Charles, passed away, and I went back to West, Texas, to go to his funeral. I stayed with my half-sister while I was down there. We talked like we did when we were younger. I told her in confidence that I was smoking wet. She really seemed concern about me, asking me how I started and if I was willing to quit or get some help. I told her I would figure it out and try to quit, but honestly I wasn't trying to stop. In fact, I was ready to go back home so I could get high again cause West, Texas. didn't sell any. We had Charles's funeral, and I stayed the weekend. I had a good time with my sister, but that was the longest weekend ever. When I went back home, I found out that Steve asked one of his good friend Rod to look after me while he was in West, Texas. And one night, I was out of it, and he walked me home. I would wonder why I called Steve. He knew everything that I was doing because Rod was reporting back, telling him everything, but it was all out of love. If I needed money or anything, he would help me. He really was concerned, and I could see that I wasn't only hurting myself, but everyone around me. He would come to Shay's house when the girls and I would sit and drink and check up on me. I knew I had plenty of support, I just needed to put it in myself to let go.

Steve finally got tired of me and cut me off and stop sending me money. I was blaming everybody else and wanted everybody to feel sorry for me, and I wasn't doing anything to help myself. I knew I was too bad off, but it's too late now because I'm hooked. I tried to stop many of times, but I found myself right back where I started. I didn't smoke at home 'cause I didn't want to see the hurt on Mark's face. I felt like it was nothing I could do, and I was disappointed with myself for starting this in the first place. Every weekend, the girls and

I would meet at Shay's house and drink. Tracy and I would sneak off and go smoke because they didn't know that I smoked except Nita. Sometimes we would bring Nita with us. She didn't smoke, but sometimes we could get her to hit it. She said it stink which it did the first time I smoked it too. It smelled like plastic burning, but now it smells so good.

One day, Tracy told me she had some good stuff. So I went to her house, and we were smoking. Then Tracy started talking in slow motion, and the room felt as if it was spinning. I thought to myself, *I'm too high.* I was trying to stay up, but my legs got weak. And I just let go. I fell, and everything just went black. I could hear Tracy calling my name, but I couldn't see her. Her voice was getting softer and softer till I couldn't hear anything anymore. Then it felt as if I peed and had a bowel movement on myself. It felt as if I was traveling in a dark tunnel, and my whole life image flashed in front of me, things in my past, just different images like a slide show going really fast. But I remember seeing it all. I just let go of the fight I had inside of me and relaxed. If I was going to die, I was ready. As I'm still in the dark, I heard Momma's voice calling me. I was thinking, *Am I dead? And why haven't I seen the light? Or was I in hell?* I didn't believe I was in heaven or hell. It was just dark.

The next thing I knew, Mark was standing over me, and I was still lying down on Tracy's floor while she was pouring milk down my throat to bring me back. I wondered, *How in the hell did he get here? And how long was I out?* She told me I passed out, and my eyes rolled in the back of my head. She thought I was dying, and she was scared. That's why she went to go get Mark. She said I was out no more than 20 minutes, but it felt like hours to me. After I got up, I checked myself to see if I had used the bathroom on myself, but I didn't. I just had a huge knot on the back of my head from when I fell and had the chills. I felt bad. I had an overdose and almost died. And here I was again, feeling shame and guilty in front of Mark. I was supposed to be the one looking after him. That's the promise I made with Sue; but here he is, taking care of me. This has to stop. I gotta beat this. But it's hard. I have been down this so many times. I just feel hopeless. The next day, they turned my lights off, so I took

De'venna over Nita's house to stay until I can get them back on. I didn't know how I was going to get them back on. I don't have a job right now, and Steve cut me off. Right now, I'm at my lowest, and this just makes me want to smoke even more. It's all about the drugs now. I thought it would get me out the funk when my kids died; but I still had the same feelings, but worst. That evening, our little group met at Shay's house like we always do on the weekend. After a couple of beers, I started crying and bending to them about my problems, my past, my lights, no job, and getting high. They didn't all know that I was getting high, and they were shocked. We all cried together and talked for hours. Nita suggested that I come to church with her in the morning. She said, "What's the worst that can happen?" So I agreed.

CHAPTER 25

As I was walking into the church, it seemed as if everyone was looking at me. It might be the shame I'm feeling inside; but I said to myself, *They already judging me*. I sat next to Nita, and Tracy was on the other side of me. As the pastor preached, I was thinking, *He's talking about me*. Every word he said, I had something in common with it. At the end of the ceremony, he asked if anyone wanted to repent and give their life to Jesus or just need a prayer to come up to the altar. At that moment, I'm sitting in my seat; and my consciousness kept saying, "Get up, get up."

I looked at Nita, and she whispered in my ear, "I will go up there with you if you want to go up there." So I said okay, and all three of us went to the altar together. The pastor asked us what we wanted. Nita was already saved, and she told him she was just up here for support.

Tracy and I said that we wanted to be saved; and he said, "Repeat after me. Dear God, I know I'm a sinner, and I ask for your forgiveness. I believe Jesus Christ is your son. I believe that he died for my sins and that you raised him to life. I want to trust him as my savior and follow him as Lord from this day forward. Guide my life and help to do your will. I pray this in the name of Jesus, Amen".

As we were praying, tears started rolling down my face, and I just broke down. It seemed as all the weight I had on my shoulders, the pain and the loses, it felt like it all just lifted away. I looked at my friends, and they were crying. The whole congregation was crying. It's a good feeling. I haven't felt this much relief ever. Chills came all over my body. I had goosebumps everywhere. It felt as God himself is hugging me; and from that moment, I knew that there is a God and is real. It's crazy because I blame God for my family's death and how he took my kids away. I was mad because I couldn't have any more kids because I had my tubes tied after De'monyea. I had so much pain, hate, and guilt inside of me. It just all went away, and I felt love and grace. I went to church with Momma when I was younger, but I never felt anything. And now I feel God's Holy Spirit all over me. I was thinking, *I never had God in my life. I have been beaten down, got right back up for another beat down, and never gave God a chance to help me back up.*

Now I'm ready to give him a chance. I want to do whatever it takes to be in the presence of God. I knew I was one of the biggest sinners; but at this moment, I felt like God has accepted me and has forgiven me for my sins, and my life has some worth to it. The whole congregation hugged us. Each of them came one by one, and I could feel the love they had for me. They really were concerned and happy for me; and it was a great feeling just knowing that others care, and you're not in this alone. After church, I made it home (De'venna was still at Nita's house). When I opened the door, I saw lights. I asked Mark "The light's on?" confused because I knew that I didn't pay the bill, and it's Sunday. The light company didn't work on today. He laughed at me and said that the neighbor next door put an extension cord in so he could plug up a lamp. To me, that was a sign from God that everything was going to be all right. Later on that night, I was lying in my bed, and I started feeling bad and sad because my children wasn't saved before they died. I was thinking, *Did my kids make it into heaven? Or do they have to suffer for the sins and mistakes I made?* Then I came across the verse in the Bible from Deuteronomy, "And the little ones that you said would be taken captive, your children who do not yet know good from bad, they will enter the land. I will give it to them, and they will take possession of it." This gave me comfort and a bit of closure. Now I really know they are in a better place.

That night, I had a dream. I was with God. I had never seen his face, but he was like a mountain to me. He put me on his shoulder and said, "You look like a grasshopper on me." Then he put me down, and I saw Jesus and he was about ten feet tall.

I looked up at him; and he said, "Welcome."

I asked, "Am I in heaven?"

He replied, "Yes." Then he looked and pointed to the right; and when I looked, I saw my boys running toward me. I started laughing and grabbed De'monyea and picked him up and hugged De'vonte so tight. When I let go, Momma, Starr, and Sue were right there beside me, and I embraced them as well. I had seen a lot of movement coming toward us, and I couldn't tell what it was because it was so far away. But it looked like a million of ants coming to us.

I asked, "What's that?"

Jesus told me, "That's all your family." I started laughing.

I said, "It's so many. I don't know most of them." I had seen both of my dads. Momma introduce me to her dad and mom. They both died before I was born. I was standing in the middle with a million or more of my people surrounding me. When I woke up, I was overwhelmed with joy. That dream was so powerful to me that it felt so real. I had no more worries about my family's afterlife, and I'm going to do my best to be a better person here. To me, that was a sign, and I know that my kids are in heaven with my family. They are all okay, and they will be waiting on me whenever time is ready for me.

Chapter 26

The next day, Tracy and I went to Nita's house with a new mind frame. We were talking about our problem, and I told them I wanted to stop smoking and change my life. We got deep in our conversation. We started crying and praying at the same time. We were praying so hard. It started lighting and thundering, and we were still praying. A lady came by, visiting Nita's mom, and said, "Y'all girls doing the right thing by praying together. Y'all praying up a storm." We started laughing, but it was true. I asked God to take the drug taste out of my mouth. I didn't need rehab, or nothing I was determined to stop smoking and God delivered it from me. I left the wet alone just like that. At the beginning, I would have these urges; but I would just pray, and they would go away until there were no more urges. When I see other people high, I wonder, *What was I thinking? How can drugs solve any of my problems? It just made things worse.* But I knew exactly what they were going through—the shame, guilt, embarrassment—and it's addicting. I pray for them and try to encourage them that if you want to quit, you can do it, nobody can't make you, and you can get all the help in the world. But if you're not ready, you're not going to stop. You got to have the will power and really want to stop. God gave me my will power, and I really wanted to stop. Just ask him to take it away and believe in him and yourself and watch it happen for you.

The next day, I got up and filed for a loan; and in the next hour, they called me back. I got approved for a five-thousand-dollar loan. That was enough money for me to pay my light bill and to put down on a car. It wasn't new, but it took me where I needed to go. I know none of this could be possible if I didn't have the Lord by my side. Tina told me to come where she was working at and applied for a job at a nursing home in the next town that was only seven miles away. I was scared because I didn't think I was going to pass my drug test 'cause it takes the wet a month to get out of your system; and things were happening so fast. Not that I had doubted him, but it's only been two weeks since I got saved. God has been blessing me left and right, and he continued blessing me because I passed my drug test and had a stable job. So I didn't have to worry about my bills. I was so thankful and happy. Life began to feel worthy like I was finally doing something right.

De'venna was doing good. She's a smart, happy girl. Now that she is getting older, I see myself in her. I sure don't want her making the same mistakes I did like my mom tried to do with me, but I fell right in her footsteps. And the cycle has to stop with De'venna. Now that I'm older, I wonder, *Did my mom see herself in me? Maybe that's why she was moody with me because she seen all the mistakes I was making*. It was hard for her to express herself because she had no one to teach her. Her mother died when she was three. I'm going to push De'venna. She has to better than I was; and whenever she needs me, I'll be right here with love, support, and advice. When I think back, there's no way she should've survive the car wreck. She was injected out of the car just like the other kids were. I believe that God left her for a reason. I don't know what's the reason. Maybe it's to save me, but I do know that I'm very blessed to have her here. People told me I'm strong and, "You always have a smile on your face. How can you smile after what you went through?" They said, "If that happened to me, I wouldn't know what to do. I'll go crazy."

I told them, "I used to say the same thing, but you never know what you will do until you actually go through it." God won't put nothing on you that you can't handle. It gets hard sometimes, but you just got to fight through it and make the best out of every situation and make God first in your life. I try to think about the good times we had together like when I took the kids to the lake, we had so much fun or doing the two-step with Sue.

I had a lot of anger and regret, but I had to learn how to forgive. I was angry with the truck driver, but now I pray for him. I know that it had to be hard for him, knowing he had something to do with a lot of kids dying. Most of all, I had to forgive myself and learn how to love myself and appreciate life. I had to let go and forgive my father. I don't know why he did the things he did; but in order to get myself right, I have to forgive all the people that wronged me and asked forgiveness to all the people that I have wronged. I know that I hurt a lot of people in my selfish ways in the past. It feels good getting all that out and just letting go of things I can't change. It gave me clarity and to just try to make it better from here forward. My message is to be the authentic person in your life. You can make your own goals and believe that God will make a way. Even at my worst, God was not ashamed of me. He accepted me, and now I live my life to serve him. I can't make no one go to church or repent their sins, he's a willing God, nothing is forced. If that's the case, I would have all my siblings in church. But just try. What's the worst that can happen. Give God a chance let him help you, and together you will become a better person.

Chapter 27

What's the odds that the same year Momma and the kids died, the oldest four grandkids were pregnant or their girlfriends were pregnant, and each one of them had their baby on the month that one of them that past on the birthday month. Also Nita had her baby exactly on De'monyea's birthday. She always gets a cake with both of their names on it. They keep my children's memory alive with their kids. Their children never met mines, but they all know everything about them. When De'vonte's classmates graduated, they had a seat for him with his picture in front of it. That made me feel so proud. He was just ten when he died, but they never forgot him. I can just imagine him sitting in that seat, getting his diploma. They did a slideshow with all his pictures. They had me crying the whole graduation. They also started a scholarship in his name. I have family and friends, especially Jim and De'vonte's classmates to keep their memories alive.

Jim doing his part like he promised. He treats De'venna as if she was his little sister. Every year, we have a dinner on their death date in their honor, it be so many people. We started a family reunion on that date. I looked back thinking, *The whole time I was partying every night, not one time did I mention God.* What I regret the most is that I should've spent more time with my kids and did more family things with them. Time was cut too fast because I wasn't there, all I was thinking about was partying and money. Another thing, I only had one picture of my baby boy. I know I have memory, but it still hurts me to find out how much of a bad mother I was to them. My mom raised my kids while I was in the streets putting everything first before them. I have a second chance with De'venna to make things right. We try to do more family things and go on vacations together.

I just try my best to make her happy and be there for her. She's my heart and really a good kid, respectful kid. I just want her to be better than me.

My girls, we still hang out every now and then. These girls are more than a friend. We are family. They are like my sisters to me. We can tell each other anything; and if one of us has a problem, we all have a problem. It's funny. Now they call me Sister Syrup; but when we all get together, we still laugh and have a good time. It took a little struggle and God's grace, but Tracy stopped smoking too. I'm so proud of her because she was on it much longer, and I know how hard it is to get off. But she said she was done and meant it. She pull herself together and took her life back. Steve is doing very well. He has another daughter after Starr, not including the other ones he already had. His children are the joy in his life. Mark saw the change and blessings in me that it motivated him, and he started going to church with me. He has always been there for me, and I thank God that he's a really nice, respectful young man.

I realize now that I was going through the pain, loses, and everything, that I was carrying it all alone. Life isn't perfect now. I still go through challenges, but I know that God is walking by my side. I was headed downhill. Nothing good was accomplished because I was trying to handle things my way; but getting saved snatched me back to reality, gave me a second chance to be a better mother and a better person in general. I find myself being in Momma's shadow often, and I believe most of my family believe that too. I try my best to be there if anyone needs advice, support, or anything with open arms. It's funny how I'm the youngest out of eight and the mother figure, but I just always try to stay positive. And if they need me, I'm there. At the time of the accident, I was twenty-six years old. The kids were ten, six, five, and three, and momma was sixty-three years old. They were all too young to go too soon. I myself was too young to go through something like that. When they died, a little part of me died too. I can't explain it. It just felt like something was missing inside of me, and it still feels that way today. I was a lost puppy, didn't know which way to go.

We were all traumatized from this. Mark couldn't ride in a car without having these anxiety attacks. He said it feels like he's having a heart attack. He went to the hospital so many times; but over time, it got better. When I drive, I try not to get close to a big truck; and every time the seatbelt gets close to my neck, I start to panic. It feels like I can't breathe, and it's cutting my neck. So whenever it gets close to my neck, I move it toward my chest. I was young and dumb, but my life experiences made me the woman I'm today. I just try to make the best of today because tomorrow is not guaranteed. Trying to be strong broke me. I had to take that mask off and add God to my life. I still have my days where I would sit in my room and cry. I know it's okay to cry sometimes. No one is perfect, and I learned to allow other people to help me. The same God that I knew when I first got saved is the same God that I serve today. He's here, waiting on us to accept and receive him. I'm not a perfect Christian, but I'm working on myself and asking God to help me be the woman that he wants me to be. I'm blessed with my new husband. He keeps me motivated and helps me stay positive. I think he loves me more than himself, and our relationship works better as a team. Not everything is perfect in our relationship either. We have our ups and downs; but like the old saying, "It's easy to fall in love but hard to stay in love." I stopped picking those young, "don't want to do anything for themselves" men. My husband is older and wants to settle down and serve God just as much as I want to. Now I'm just trying to live life one day at a time and serve God the best I can. I'm blessed to have my family and friends.

Forever Young

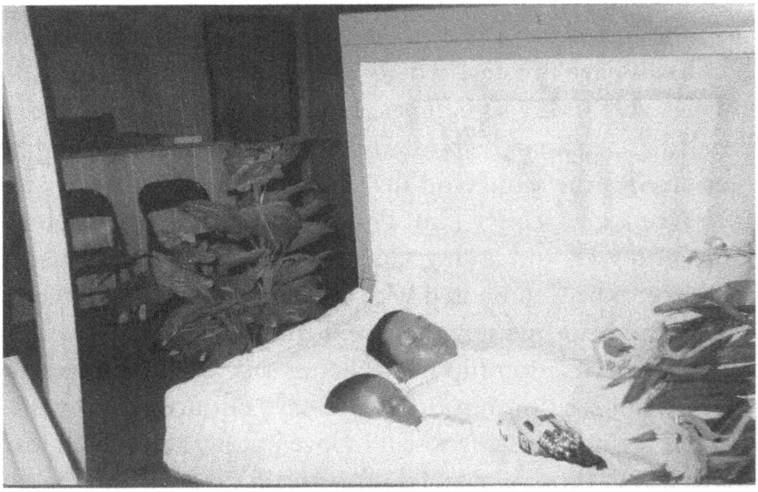

I remember at the lake up under the sun. A lot of people were there, but we had so much fun. I never thought death will take you so soon, and you will be forever young. Forever young you will be. Forever young, you without me. Forever young, you will remain ten and three. I'm so lost what can I do? Nothing, but know that I will forever love you.

CPSIA information can be obtained
at www.ICGtesting.com
Printed in the USA
LVHW031656080121
675851LV00002B/246

9 781098 061418